SMALL TALK

SMALL TALK

ACTIVITIES FOR LANGUAGE DEVELOPMENT IN PRESCHOOL LEARNERS

Charles Reid Taylor

ROWMAN & LITTLEFIELD
Lanham • Boulder • New York • London

Published by Rowman & Littlefield
An imprint of The Rowman & Littlefield Publishing Group, Inc.
4501 Forbes Boulevard, Suite 200, Lanham, Maryland 20706
www.rowman.com

6 Tinworth Street, London, SE11 5AL, United Kingdom

British Library Cataloguing in Publication Information Available

Library of Congress Cataloging-in-Publication Data

Names: Taylor, Charles Reid, 1954– author.
Title: Small talk : activities for language development in preschool
  learners / Charles Reid Taylor.
Description: Lanham, Maryland : Rowman & Littlefield, 2022. | Includes
  bibliographical references. | Summary: "Small Talk provides simple,
  powerful activities involving arts and crafts, food, and game
  activities that are well within the abilities of preschool children"—
  Provided by publisher.
Identifiers: LCCN 2021032081 (print) | LCCN 2021032082 (ebook) | ISBN
  9781475862157 (cloth) | ISBN 9781475862164 (paperback) | ISBN
  9781475862171 (epub)
Subjects: LCSH: Children—Language. | Language arts (Preschool)—Activity
  programs.
Classification: LCC LB1139.L3 T38 2022 (print) | LCC LB1139.L3 (ebook) |
  DDC 372.6—dc23
LC record available at https://lccn.loc.gov/2021032081
LC ebook record available at https://lccn.loc.gov/2021032082

This book is dedicated to all the young learners
who come to us with instructions.

CONTENTS

CONTENTS

ACKNOWLEDGMENTS

The author wishes to thank each of the following people for their love, support, caring, and inspiration throughout the challenging times as this book was being written:

Dr. Carol Nancy Fleres—thank you for insisting that I pursue the publication of *Small Talk*.

Carla Marie Giannobile—thank you for your photography expertise.

Romulo Avila—thank you for asking me, "So, where's *your* book?"

Uriel Delgado—thank you for painting the milk cartons for the bowling activity photo.

The descendants of Lula Entzminger

The late Thomas Gerald and Audrey Taylor

The late Dr. Louise Entminger Taylor

Adrienne C. Taylor Hall, Wayne Gerald Taylor, and Captain Dwayne Rashawn Taylor

Robert M. Mason Jr.—thank you for your kind words of encouragement.

Julie Monfleury and her son, Jonathan Monfleury

The late Angela Maxwell

Joanne Z. Bruno and Richard Sentipal—thank you for leading me to Zelda.

Zelda Schuster—thank you for leading me to Dr. Zelefsky.

Dr. Patricia Yacobacci—thank you for standing by me through my doctoral studies.

Xavier Luis Garcia and David P. Howard

Veny Delgado

Jose Angel Martinez

The late Brian Novack Lindsey

Dr. Robert Kenneth Gale and Dr. Michael Zelefsky

Prof. Ruth Pachtman—thank you for leading me to speech-language pathology.

INTRODUCTION

Small Talk: Activities for Language Development in Preschool Learners is a creative format for teaching basic language skills to young children. Through the use of craft activities, easy food recipes, science projects, and card games, language teaching/learning takes on a new dimension. The child becomes an active participant in her/his language growth, rather than taking the passive role while memorizing language structures by means of uninspiring drills. This multisensory program helps preschool language learners develop receptive and expressive language skills. The included activities also assist in developing temporal-spatial concepts, visual memory and sequencing skills, and visual-motor proficiency.

Presenting basic language-learning concepts both auditorily and visually provides a logical basis for language teaching. Success within the academic setting is closely linked to the development of specific auditory and visual attention and memory skills. Both auditory and visual attention are vital in the learning process as the child attends to the teacher's step-by-step instructions for completing each of the *Small Talk* activities. Those skills are reinforced when the young learner understands that there are positive results that come with attentive behavior. The same skills are needed as the child is expected to absorb curriculum content for math, reading, writing, social studies, etc.

Auditory memory skills are called upon when the child orally reviews the sequence of steps needed to complete any one of the *Small Talk* activities. Visual memory skills come into play as the child follows the teacher's lead during activities. Some teachers might even direct the child to close her/his eyes as the teacher reviews the steps taken to complete the activity, as "revisualization" gives the child an opportunity to further develop visual memory and sequencing skills.

Development of receptive and expressive language skills takes place when the child begins to comprehend the basic concepts needed to complete a *Small Talk* activity. As the child hears the verbal directives and completes the activity, words take on a brand-new dimension. Furthermore, motor activity, coupled with adult verbalization, can provide an opportunity for significant language comprehension and expression.

The *Small Talk* activities encourage the child to take on an active role in her/his language learning. In so doing, she/he is given practice in planning, comprehending, and, for most of the projects, producing a finished product that is her/his own. This will go a long way in helping the child develop confidence and a desire to remain focused on learning. The *Small Talk* activities are designed to appeal to the child's play instinct as a means of stimulating her/his desire to learn more and more.

Each activity has been written in a clear step-by-step fashion so that busy classroom teachers will find the directions easy to follow and parents will be able to perform the projects in the home as well. Moreover, the speech-language pathologist searching for new treatment ideas will be able to enhance therapy by using *Small Talk*.

Small Talk presents ideas for carrying out experience-based activities to facilitate the development of basic language skills. Each activity contains a list of easy-to-obtain materials and/or ingredients. There is also a set of procedures intended to make each activity easy to conduct by the busy classroom teacher or speech-language pathologist, or the parent who has little or no formal training in education or language development. Each activity concludes with "Small Talk Suggestions," specific ideas that the teacher or parent can use to stimulate a language-building conversation. The activities have been designed to maximize their potential for encouraging communication between the language learner and a trusted adult language model.

The primary purpose of this book is to present suggestions for the use of everyday materials to teach and/or provide for basic language development within a meaningful social context. Suggestions are provided to guide the adult in how to present the activity in as natural an environment as possible. Furthermore, as the child develops competency in vocabulary and concepts, she/he may be expected to add linguistic patterns and to initiate requests for what she/he wants, both within the activities and at other times. She/he may be directed to ask for something or the adult may hide what the child wants in order to stimulate question initiation. A hesitant child can be supported by modeling what to say. Each *Small Talk* activity is designed to provide the learner with opportunities to interact with the teacher as the language model in a natural and meaningful context.

①

SUGGESTED APPLICATION

The activities in this book were developed in an effort to fill a real need expressed by in-service and preservice teachers, as well as parents. Motivated to encourage the transfer of language skills from my therapy room to the classroom and home, these caring individuals sought materials and activities that were inexpensive and easy to use while working to facilitate language development among preschoolers, in particular, and older children whose developmental ages were significantly lower than their chronological ages. In response, I began sharing my language development ideas, and designing more activities for myself and other professionals and nonprofessionals to implement both in and outside the therapeutic setting. The *Small Talk* set of activities was born of this desire to share ideas for the benefit of preschool children.

The activities in this book were designed and originally used to supplement language therapy for children presenting with a wide range of disabilities: autism, cognitive impairment, learning disability, hearing impairment. I also see application of the *Small Talk* activities with preschool children who are not classified learners, but might benefit from language-enrichment activities.

Parents, special educators, general educators, as well as speech-language pathologists should have no difficulty conducting the *Small Talk* activities, which may be useful in facilitating the development of age-appropriate receptive and expressive language skills, as well as helping with auditory attention, auditory memory, sequencing, classification describing, following directions, predicting, reasoning, problem-solving, role-playing, eye-hand coordination, finger dexterity, basic concepts, turn-taking, and visual memory skills.

PLANNING AND PRESENTING THE ACTIVITIES

The *Small Talk* activities consist of no-tech materials and ingredients that may be found in most homes and classrooms. If anything must be purchased, such items should be readily available at the local stationery store, a supermarket, or the corner store/bodega.

Each activity opens with the title of the specific project and is followed by a chart showing communication skills. These skills include: Auxiliary Verbs; Cognitive Skills; Commentary, Questioning, Requesting; Concept Development; Future Tense (will); Giving and Following Verbal Directives; Modals; Negation; Past Tense Verbs; Pragmatics; Present Progressive Tense; Present Tense Verbs; Requesting Assistance; Questions (asking and/or responding); Sequencing Skills; Vocabulary Development; Vocabulary Review. For each activity chart, there will be a check mark (√) beside the skills that are specifically highlighted in that particular activity.

Following the chart is "Time Needed for Activity." The length of time required for completion of each activity will vary according to the complexity of the activity selected and the degree to which the child's oral communication is stimulated by the activity, as well as the adult language model's ability to engage and focus the child's attention. Nevertheless, an estimation of time needed for the activity has been provided, based upon my experience with the language projects.

Following "Time Needed for Activity" is my estimation of the "Difficulty Level." Based upon my repeated use of the various activities in therapy, three levels of difficulty have been identified:

- Easy: little to no intricate fine motor abilities required
- Intermediate: best for young learners with some experience with fine motor control/coordination
- Challenging: may require more than usual hand-over-hand assistance with children who possess little experience handling arts and crafts and/or cooking/eating utensils

Next, there is a listing of suggested vocabulary words and basic concepts that can be highlighted throughout the activity to provide for language stimulation among the children. It is entirely up to the teacher to determine which words and concepts will be included in the activity. She/he should feel free to use all or some of the suggestions or to add to the printed listing.

After suggested vocabulary and concepts, there is a listing of simple materials needed for the project, along with step-by-step procedures as guidance for completion of the activity. I advise that the teacher take the time to perform the activity prior to introducing it to the children so that there is a completed example of the finished product to show to the children.

Under "Small Talk Suggestions," there are numerous ideas for comments or questions that the teacher might use while interacting with the children a) before actually performing the activity, b) during the activity, and c) after the activity has been completed. In parentheses after these suggestions are specific language objectives/skills (see the charts) that can be targeted throughout the activity. For example, if a child presents with difficulty comprehending and/or expressing present progressive tense, it is recommended that the teacher locate an activity in *Small Talk* that has "Present Progressive Tense" checked in the chart at the beginning of the activity. In the "Small Talk Suggestions," there will be at least one example of a sentence that can be used by the teacher for language stimulation of the child within the context of a natural and meaningful activity. Teachers are strongly advised to reach into their imaginations for further comments or questions that are intended to stimulate the communication objective within the involved child.

Finally, for each of the activities, suggestions are given to teachers and other caring adults to help facilitate the development of language skills in the young learner. Each of these suggestions might be shared with other adults who work with the child, such as other school personnel, parents, administrators, etc.

It is not mandatory that all of the activities be performed. In addition, there is no particular sequence in which to approach the activities. Most importantly, activity selection should be based upon the specific needs and interests of the individual child. For example, educators and speech-language pathologists making activity selections for a child are advised to review the child's individualized education plan (IEP) when working with a child who is a classified learner. Parents and teachers are urged to make necessary adaptations of the materials in order to meet a child's unique needs. It is, therefore, important that anyone who intends to use these activities should review the entire activity, especially the "Small Talk Suggestions," prior to beginning the actual activity with a young language learner. The "Small Talk Suggestions" list should be viewed as a set of ideas intended to spark the imagination of the adult who is working with the child as a language model. The adult is encouraged to adapt the suggestions to suit the unique needs of the child.

While the "Small Talk Suggestions" vary from activity to activity, there are additional things teachers can do for all the projects with only slight changes, depending upon the selected activity, such as the following:

1. After the activity has been completed, encourage the children to tell someone who was not present what the class did for the activity. This may include a child who was absent, another teacher, a member of the housekeeping or janitorial staff, the principal, a parent volunteer, etc. Look for correct sequencing of the steps and materials/ingredients. Try to keep prompting to a minimum. (Pragmatics; Sequencing Skills)

2. Create a situation wherein a utensil or an ingredient integral to the activity is absent or otherwise out of the child's reach. This may stimulate the child to ask for the item, to ask for help. (Requesting Assistance; Vocabulary Development; Commenting, Questioning, Requesting)

3. Look for opportunities to vocally highlight specific vocabulary words/concepts throughout the activity. (Vocabulary Development)

4. Try a variation on the activity by setting up all of the tools and ingredients for the activity on a table in front of the children. Tell them what to do, step-by-step, allowing them time to perform each step on their own. (Sequencing Skills)

5. Take photographs of the children as they perform key steps of the selected activity. From whatever number of photos are taken, choose the three to five photos that best illustrate the sequence representing the activity. Print those photos, and mount each on its own sheet of firm card stock, using rubber cement. Trim the card stock excess to the size of the photo. Now, the teacher can use the activity cards for a sequencing task. Mix up the cards, then encourage a child to put them in the correct order. The teacher may elect to use the same cards for subsequent classes over the next years, but it is highly recommended that new photo sets be created for each new class of children. Authentic materials (materials depicting people, pets, etc., familiar to the child) will undoubtedly have more meaning to the children using them. (Sequencing Skills)

THE IMPORTANCE OF EARLY CHILDHOOD LANGUAGE LEARNING

Age-appropriate language skill in very young children is important to their growth, both academically and socially. The child who cannot adequately comprehend the teacher's instructions or participate in classroom discussions is unable to fully take advantage of the educational opportunities placed before her/him. If she/he cannot understand what her/his peers are saying during typical playtime activities or express herself/himself appropriately on the playground at recess time, she/he will be isolated and will miss out on the social growth experiences that are invaluable to the stimulation of the young developing brain. Caring adults are key figures in the process of intervening when a child needs assistance in developing her/his ability to use language skills in the home, school environment, and larger community. Chief among these caring adults are the child's teachers and parents.

Teachers and parents have the huge responsibility of raising and teaching children in this challenging era. The pressures of seeing to the general welfare, the health, and the safety of very young children is often an overwhelming experience when taken seriously. While numerous professionals have, as their scope of practice, the job of monitoring the medical, academic, social, and emotional needs of the developing child, it remains that classroom teachers and parents are the central members on the child-development team.

Teacher and parent involvement in the language development of the young child cannot be overemphasized. Typically, it is teachers and parents who are frequently called upon to encourage transfer of language skills beyond the school building and into the homes and the community. Furthermore, teachers and parents have the ability to observe children's language skills in a variety of settings that others may not. This affords them the opportunity to take special notice of how well a child understands what is said to her/him (receptive language) and how well she/he uses oral language to express thoughts, needs, and desires to others (expressive language).

Unfortunately, language problems in many young children are not diagnosed until the child has already experienced several years of failure and frustration in school. Many parents and teachers do not realize that there is a problem until there appears a record of failing grades, especially in reading. Some parents are so focused on daily living issues or careers that they have left the teaching responsibilities solely to teachers. Some teachers are so burdened with large classes and accountability issues that they may not notice the subtler symptoms that suggest or indicate a language problem. Still others may notice a problem but assume that the child will simply grow out of it.

Children with language problems do not grow out of it. They require intervention. They need treatment. They require caring adults who are able to provide language models for developing brains to absorb. They need caregivers who are willing to stimulate the child in ways that compensate for any language problems they may have and to help the child learn how to use oral language skills within a social context. They also need an adult who is aware of what the signs of a possible language problem are. What are the characteristics or symptoms of a language problem?

SYMPTOMS OF LANGUAGE IMPAIRMENT

Children with a language impairment often look as "normal" as any other child, but looks can sometimes be deceiving. Following is a list of behaviors/symptoms for teachers to be aware of.[1] Please keep in mind that the occasional observation of one or two of these symptoms may not be the sign of an actual language problem. Whatever behavior is observed, one should look for a pattern of this behavior. Does it occur in a variety of settings or just in one? Is it only seen at school? There are many reasons why a child may appear unable to pay attention when he or she is being spoken to. He/She may be sleepy or sick. Or perhaps bored. In other words, it is important for caring adults to look at the child's environment to explain behavioral concerns before putting the onus or placing a diagnostic label on the young child.

A RECEPTIVE LANGUAGE PROBLEM

When a child has a receptive language problem, she/he has difficulty understanding what is said to her/him. Note the following symptoms:

- Many of these children have an unusually difficult time learning and remembering new words as compared to other children of the same age. They are unable to understand them or use them appropriately. It seems that shortly after exposure to the new word(s), these youngsters may have difficulty recalling the words and/or their meaning(s).

- They sometimes exhibit a blank expression when spoken to, showing little if any interest in the communication of others. They appear expressionless because they simply do not understand what is being said to them.

- These children almost always have poor memories, especially when they are given directions to perform a specific task with more than one or two steps. They may remember only the last step and not recall what was to be done first and second.

- They may respond to comments and questions inappropriately. These children may be very aware that the adult's question requires some sort of response. They may want to please the authority figure, but they are not certain how to respond to the question that they do not understand. In their attempt to "wing it," these children end up responding inappropriately, saying things that may be interpreted by adults as bizarre.

- They often lack comprehension of simple nursery rhymes and/or jokes. Many jokes, riddles, and nursery rhymes rely on the listener's understanding of the multiple meanings of various words, idioms, and the slang expressions or phrases often associated with different cultures in a given community. While these expressions serve to enrich the language, children who have language comprehension and use problems cannot appreciate such enrichment in the same way that their age-mates may.

- They may become easily frustrated with conversation. In the typical, quick-paced give-and-take of most conversations between two or more people, children with language comprehension problems get lost. They cannot keep up as they try to process not only all that is being said but their own responses, as well.

- They tire easily during activities that require listening and/or concentrated mental effort. Actually, they may be bored with hearing so much, yet understanding so little of what is going on around them. These children are working hard to comprehend, but they get so little out of the effort. This can leave them exhausted.

- They may repeat the speaker's question or comment before responding. This is a frequently observed behavior among children who have language comprehension problems. It appears that they are using this strategy to help them process meaning from the spoken language of others around them. This only causes more frustration because by the time these children have processed the adult's question, and then their own response, the conversation may have moved on, or the child's conversation partner has become disinterested in continuing the conversation.

- Especially in the classroom setting, the language-impaired child may not respond consistently to instructions given to the class. Depending upon the complexity of the verbal directive, this child may have more difficulty at one time or another. A common strategy that these children adopt is to "hang back" a bit and watch how the other children in the classroom are responding, then copy their actions. She/he may not have understood what the teacher said, but suddenly the other children take out their crayons, so she/he takes out crayons, too. Ten other kids in the room cannot all be wrong.

- They can be highly distracted by sounds in and around the room that unimpaired children seem able to ignore. Sometimes, these children are unable to screen out or ignore competing auditory stimuli. Whereas the typically developing child has no problem attending to the adult's language amid the sounds of shuffling papers, the dog barking, the refrigerator motor, the television, etc., many children with language problems cannot focus nearly as easily. All of these sounds are competing for the child's attention.
- They seem to tune out spoken language. This sometimes gives adults the impression that these children are ignoring them, being willful and uncooperative, when the problem may actually be that they just do not understand enough of what is being said to them.

AN EXPRESSIVE LANGUAGE PROBLEM

When a child has difficulty using oral language skills to communicate needs and thoughts to others, she/he is said to have an expressive language problem. Following are some symptoms of such impairment:

- This child may appear to be unusually quiet or shy. Sometimes, in a large, over-crowded classroom, this child can become the busy teacher's dream. He does not cause trouble. He is the good boy. Actually, the child may be quiet because he is unable to use language age-appropriately.
- They sometimes ramble when speaking, not making much or any sense. These kids often have problems in organizing their thoughts. During speaking, their lack of organization is reflected in their spoken language abilities.
- They frequently use words incorrectly. If these children do not comprehend words appropriately, it is a sure bet that they will not use them appropriately to express their needs either.
- They may have frequent bouts of tantrums as their inability to express themselves proves frustrating during moments of stress.
- They tend to produce shorter sentences than their unimpaired age-mates. It is not unusual for these children to rely upon a few simple sentence types because they have failed to learn more age-appropriate types to communicate their needs.
- They may appear to be dysfluent, using frequent pauses or "filler" words, such as "you know," "like," "um," "uh," or "well." Sometimes, adults misinterpret this

behavior as some type of stuttering. This behavior may, in fact, be the result of children attempting to word-find as they are speaking.

- They may overgeneralize an already limited vocabulary. For example, these children may learn what a dog is but will then refer to all furry, four-legged animals as "dog," or all liquids in a cup are referred to as "juice" instead of what it might actually be.

Can the presence of only one of these symptoms be indicative of a language problem? None of these characteristics alone necessarily indicates a language problem. When a pattern of difficulty appears in a variety of communicative settings, there may be a problem that requires intervention. When several symptoms are manifest, they may indicate the possibility of a language impairment that does, in fact, warrant further examination by a professional. Please keep in mind that any one of several different conditions, such as hunger, lack of sleep, illness, or emotional stress may cause a child to present with the mentioned symptoms.

SIMPLE STRATEGIES FOR DEVELOPING LANGUAGE SKILLS IN YOUNG CHILDREN

Here are some tips for parents and teachers who want to become facilitators of language development for their young children:

- Find some time every day to read to your child. This will give her/him an opportunity on a daily basis to hear the grammatically intact language that she/he is expected to understand and use. She/he will get to hear the sounds associated with the language and associate words with pictures and concepts. It does not have to be a long, drawn-out story. Reading a brief story is far better than no reading at all. If you think the child is unable to tolerate a long story, just look at the pictures together and make up a short story of a sentence or two for each page.
- Try parallel talk with your child. As your child engages in a given activity, talk about what she/he is doing. Do a brief commentary out loud on the child's actions and what is being acted on. In this way, you are providing words and sentences within a meaningful context.
- Use self-talk. This is similar to parallel talk, but instead of talking to the child about what she/he is doing, you talk about what *you* are doing. This is ideal during cooking activities, household chores, taking a walk through the neighborhood, etc.
- Keep your verbal output simple. Some believe that children who are still developing their language skills need to hear adults talking, talking, and talking. Such jabbering is unnecessary and may actually be preventing the child from using his or her own verbal skills to attempt a comment. Use simple sentences that do not

overwhelm the child. Where appropriate, pair your words with gestures that will help convey your meaning to the child more clearly.

- Avoid "baby-talk" at all costs. Under absolutely no circumstances is it cute or adorable to model inappropriate language patterns for the young child who is in the process of developing age-appropriate language skills. This is especially true for the child who is known to have or is suspected of having a language impairment. What this child needs are good examples of the language that she/he is expected to understand and use, not bombardment with invented words used in grammatically defective sentences.

- Expand the child's language. If the child tends to communicate using only one-word utterances to convey sentence-like meaning, then use that word in a sentence. For example:

  ○ Child (reaching for a cookie): Cookie!
  ○ Parent: Sean wants a cookie. I want a cookie, too.

- Follow the child's lead. If you and the child are playing with a particular toy, then suddenly the child appears more interested in having some juice, do not feel compelled to stay with the toy. Go with the child's interest. Prepare some juice, but use that time to talk about the juice and expand on any words the child uses.

- Respond to the child even if you are not certain what she/he has said. Sometimes, the child's speech may be unclear. That is no reason to not respond. Given the context of the child's utterance, take a guess at what you think the child is referring to, and respond accordingly. Yes, you do run the risk of guessing incorrectly, but the child still knows that you were listening. At least she/he knows that you are willing to listen and that what she/he says matters to you.

- Do not demand perfection. In the early stages of language development, the child needs to be confident that what is said to you matters more than how it may have been said.

- Get down on the child's level, literally! Imagine how frustrating it must be to little children who must always crane their necks upward during conversations with adults. When talking with a child, move down to her/him by kneeling, resting on your haunches, sitting on the floor next to the child, or sitting on a child's chair. This will have the effect of letting the child see how you form words and sentences, how your facial expressions match your mood, and chiefly, how what she/he has to say is important enough for you to stop what you are doing and listen.

- Avoid asking the child lots of questions that require only a "yes" or "no" response. When appropriate, try asking a question like, "What is happening to the . . . ?" You might elect to make a comment, such as, "Tell me about that . . . "

- Use your voice inflection in an animated way to vocally highlight new vocabulary or language structures that need to be emphasized for the child. Sometimes, children with language learning problems have difficulty focusing their attention on what a parent or teacher is saying. During your conversations with the child, try to be more interesting than the child's distractions. The way you express yourself with your voice and body language can help focus the child's attention on you as the main figure during all interactions, with only minimal or no distraction by extraneous auditory and/or visual stimuli.

NOTE

1. "Preschool Language Disorders," American Speech-Language-Hearing Association, accessed February 8, 2021, https://www.asha.org/public/speech/disorders/preschool-language-disorders/#signs.

DEVELOPMENTAL MILESTONES FOR SPEECH AND LANGUAGE

The preschool classroom teacher is uniquely qualified to assist in the identification of a child who may need referral for assessment for possible language impairment. This is the education professional who spends the most contact time with the child and becomes best acquainted with the child's developmental stages across a variety of skills. It is the teacher who has ample opportunity to observe her/his young charges as they not only interact with the teacher, the central figure within the school environment, but with the child's age-mates and other school personnel, such as the physical education teacher, classroom aides, teacher interns, etc. It is by means of keen observation that the teacher is able to identify a child who may be in need of screening and/or diagnostic testing for a language impairment that has the potential of impacting the affected child's academic, social, and behavioral growth.

How does a busy classroom teacher go about the task of identifying a child with a language impairment? What is the foundation of the teacher's knowledge base? Every teacher needs to have a firm understanding of ages and stages, developmental milestones for speech and language. Every preschool teacher charged with the responsibility of identifying a child with a possible language disorder and making a referral to the speech-language pathologist (SLP) and/or the child study team needs to be well versed in typical development of children. Such a knowledge base will provide vital baseline information as the teacher interacts with the young learners in his/her care. What follows is some basic content pertaining to the speech and language developmental milestones of children within the chronological age ranges of 0–6 months through 6–7 years of age.[1] This information should serve as a set of guidelines to the speech and language growth expectations observed among typically developing children.

0–6 MONTHS

Speech and Language Skills

Children within this age range should be expected to:

- repeat sounds during vocal play
- make cooing, gurgling, "pleasure" sounds
- produce differentiated cries to express different needs
- smile upon social approach by familiar persons
- recognize voice of familiar persons
- localize to sound by turning head to the source of the sound
- attend to speech
- utter speech sounds /p/, /b/, /m/ during vocal play
- utter sounds or gestures to indicate wants

Motor Skills

Children within this age range should be expected to:

- smile
- elevate head and shoulders from a prone position
- sit while using hands for support
- reach for objects with one hand, usually missing the object
- visually track objects and people

7–12 MONTHS

Speech and Language Skills

Children within this age range should be expected to:

- understand "hot" and "no"
- respond appropriately to simple verbal directives
- understand and respond appropriately to his/her name
- attend to and imitate some sounds
- recognize words for common objects within his/her environment (e.g., milk, spoon, shoe)
- babble, using long and short groups of sounds
- produce a sing-song intonation pattern when babbling
- imitate some adult-like speech-sounds (phonemes) and intonation patterns
- gradually produce more speech-sounds than crying to seek attention

- utter an extensive variety of sounds during babbling
- listen attentively when spoken to
- approximate speech-sounds
- slowly transition from babbling to jargoning
- intentionally use speech
- utter nouns
- evidence an expressive vocabulary of 1 to 3 words

Motor Skills

Children within this age range should be able to:

- crawl on stomach
- stand or walk with assistance
- attempt to feed self with spoon
- push self up to sitting position
- imitate adult gestures during speech
- employ a smooth continuous movement to reach for an object
- sit unsupported
- drink from a cup
- pull self to a standing position, using furniture
- hold own bottle
- play ball with a partner
- enjoy games like peek-a-boo and pat-a-cake
- employ a primitive grip for writing
- cooperate with dressing (puts foot out for shoe, places arms through sleeves, etc.)

13–18 MONTHS

Speech and Language Skills

Children in this age range should be expected to:

- consistently produce adult-like intonation patterns
- make utterances often consisting of echolalia and jargon
- omit many initial speech-sounds
- omit almost all final sounds from words
- rely upon oral communication that consists chiefly of unintelligible speech
- follow simple directions
- receptively identify 1 to 3 body parts accurately
- use an expressive vocabulary consisting of about 3 to 20+ words (nouns)

- combine gestures and speech to communicate
- use speech and gestures to request specific objects

Motor Skills

Children within this age range should be able to:

- point to recognized/desired objects
- run, though frequently falling
- imitate gestures
- remove clothing
- make attempts to pull zippers up and down

19–24 MONTHS

Speech and Language Skills

Children within this age range should be able to:

- produce real words with greater frequency than jargon
- use an expressive vocabulary consisting of approximately 50 to 100+ words
- use a receptive vocabulary consisting of approximately 300+ words
- combine nouns and verbs in short phrases
- begin using pronouns
- consistently use appropriate rising intonation for questions
- be approximately 25–50 percent intelligible to strangers
- respond appropriately to "What's that?" questions
- enjoy listening activities (storytelling)
- understand and express names of at least 5 body parts
- accurately utter names of familiar objects

Motor Skills

Children within this age range should be able to:

- walk with no assistance
- string beads
- enjoy manipulating clay (Play-Doh)
- pick up objects from floor without falling
- ascend and descend stairs with assistance

- climb and stand on chair to obtain desired object
- insert a key into a lock
- stand on one foot with assistance
- make a tower consisting of 3 cubes

2–3 YEARS

Speech and Language Skills

Children within this age range should be able to:

- use speech that is approximately 50–75 percent intelligible
- comprehend number concepts, such as "one" and "all"
- verbalize toilet needs before, during, or after the act
- request desired items by name
- point to pictured items in a book when named by teacher or parent
- identify several body parts
- respond appropriately to simple questions
- enjoy short stories, songs, nursery rhymes
- combine 1 to 2 words to ask a question
- speak, using 3- to 4-word phrases
- increasingly use some prepositions, articles, present progressive verbs, regular plurals, contractions, irregular past tense forms
- possess a receptive vocabulary of approximately 500 to 900+ words
- possess an expressive vocabulary of approximately 50 to 250+ words and growing
- express short sentences, but produce them with multiple grammatical errors
- understand most of what is said to her/him
- produce vowel sounds correctly
- utter initial speech-sounds correctly most of the time
- often omit medial speech-sounds
- often omit or substitute final speech-sounds
- utter approximately 27 speech-sounds

Motor Skills

Children within this age range should be expected to:

- ambulate with characteristic toddler movement
- ascend and descend stairs without assistance
- balance on one foot for one second

- turn pages of a book one by one (sometimes two or three at a time)
- fold paper in half imitatively
- build a tower of 6 blocks
- paint, using whole arm movement
- drink from a full glass, using one hand
- undress self

3–4 YEARS

Speech and Language

Children within this age range should be expected to:

- comprehend object functions
- comprehend opposites (up/down, big/little, etc.)
- follow 2- and 3-part verbal directives
- ask and appropriately respond to simple "wh" questions (who, what, when, where, why)
- insist upon detailed responses from adults when asking questions and making demands
- use words to express emotions
- repeat 6- to 13-syllable sentences with accuracy
- produce sentences consisting of 4 to 6 words
- identify objects by name (mostly noun + verb combinations)
- understand concepts of past and future
- use receptive vocabulary of approximately 1,200 to 2,000+ words
- use expressive vocabulary of approximately 800 to 1,500+ words
- accurately use at least 50 percent of consonants and consonant blends in speech
- use grammatically correct language more consistently
- speak about an event with appropriate sequencing of events
- engage in long conversations
- utter some contractions, irregular plurals, future tense verbs, and contractions
- consistently use regular plurals, possessives, and simple past tense verbs

Motor Skills

Children in this age range should be expected to:

- kick a ball forward
- turn pages of a storybook, one page at a time

- use scissors appropriately
- participate in gross motor activities involved in most children's playground games
- unbutton clothing
- grasp a crayon, using a mature grip with thumb and fingers, not a fist
- trace shapes
- put on shoes (maybe not the correct foot, yet)
- ride a tricycle independently
- build a tower of blocks consisting of 9 cubes
- alternate feet while ascending and descending stairs
- jump in place with both feet together
- use a spoon to eat without spilling

4–5 YEARS

Speech and Language Skills

Children within this age range should be expected to:

- count up to 5
- comprehend number concepts up to at least 5
- identify approximately 3 colors
- use a receptive vocabulary of approximately 2,000 words
- use an expressive vocabulary consisting of approximately 900 to 2,000+ words
- respond correctly to questions about object function
- utter sentences that are grammatically intact
- utter sentences consisting of 4 to 8 words
- request definitions of words
- utter consonants with about 90 percent accuracy
- produce speech that is intelligible to strangers
- speak about remote experiences, such as events that took place at school, home, etc.
- attend to a story, then respond correctly to questions about the story

Motor Skills

Children within this age range should be expected to:

- throw a ball with direction
- pour liquid from a pitcher without spilling
- toilet selves independently
- walk on a straight line

- consistently grasp a writing utensil with mature grip
- draw circles, squares, diamonds
- take part in cutting and pasting activities

5-6 YEARS

Speech and Language Skills

Children within this age range should be expected to:

- label at least 6 basic colors
- label at least 3 basic shapes
- accurately follow 3-step verbal directives
- ask "how" questions
- use past tense and future tense correctly
- use conjunctions appropriately during spontaneous discourse
- have a receptive vocabulary of about 13,000 words
- appropriately name opposites
- say the names of the week in correct sequence
- engage in conversation, exchanging information and asking questions appropriately
- increasingly express details in conversations
- sing entire songs and recite nursery rhymes correctly
- easily engage in conversation with other children and adults
- use sentences that are almost always grammatically correct

Motor Skills

Children within this age range should be expected to:

- do somersaults
- use scissors to cut on a line
- print capital letters
- use a knife to cut food
- tie own shoes
- build complex structures with blocks/Legos
- ride a bike, roller-skate, jump rope
- button clothing
- play catch with a ball
- use crayons to color with precision

6–7 YEARS

Speech and Language Skills

Children within this age range should be expected to:

- name letters, numbers, currency accurately
- comprehend "left" and "right"
- use a receptive vocabulary of about 20,000 words
- comprehend most concepts of time
- recite the entire alphabet
- count from 1 to 100 with accuracy
- correctly use morphologic markers

Motor Skills

Children within this age range should be expected to:

- enjoy gross motor activities, such as running, jumping, skipping, racing, playing tag
- draw a recognizable man, tree, house
- cut out simple shapes
- dress self completely without assistance
- walk on a balance beam
- color within the lines
- brush teeth independently

Because there exists great variance among developing children, any discussion of developmental sequences must be considered with caution. Rigid application of age and stage approximations is inappropriate. Even typically developing children have been known to develop certain skills more quickly or more slowly than others. Not every child will start to babble or jargon at the exact same point in their growth. That does not mean there is necessarily a language or other disorder affecting the child; however, if a teacher observes a gap in a child's developmental milestones, there may be a problem that needs to be addressed by other professionals, individuals trained in diagnostic and therapeutic procedures pertaining to speech and language skills, gross and fine motor skills, feeding disorders, etc.

NOTE

1. "CDC's Developmental Milestones," Centers for Disease Control and Prevention, last modified June 10, 2020, https://www.cdc.gov/ncbddd/actearly/milestones/index.html.

EASY ACTIVITIES

The following activities (Difficulty Level #1) are considered relatively easy for young learners to perform, as they require little to no intricate fine motor skills.

A TASTY GUESSING GAME

Figure 3.1.   A Tasty Guessing Game.

√	COMMUNICATION SKILL	√	COMMUNICATION SKILL
√	Auxiliary Verbs	√	Pragmatics
√	Cognitive Skills	√	Present Progressive Tense
√	Commentary, Questioning, Requesting	√	Present Tense Verbs
√	Concept Development		Requesting Assistance
√	Future Tense (will)	√	Questions (asking and/or responding)
	Giving and Following Verbal Directives		Sequencing Skills
√	Modals	√	Vocabulary Development
√	Negation	√	Vocabulary Review
√	Past Tense Verbs		

Time Needed for Activity: Approximately 30 minutes
Difficulty Level: #1
Suggested Concepts and Vocabulary:

- names of various fruits

    ○ apple
    ○ banana
    ○ orange
    ○ pear
    ○ peach
    ○ cherry
    ○ melon
    ○ lemon

- chunks
- cut
- taste
- select
- pieces
- slices
- sweet
- sour
- bitter
- color words associated with the fruits selected for this project

Materials:

- 2 of each fruit: apples, bananas, oranges, pears, pineapples, peaches, melons, lemons (and any other desired fruits)
- bite-sized chunks of apple, banana, orange, pear, pineapple, peach, melon, lemon, etc.
- a small bowl for each of the fruit chunks once sliced into chunks
- spoons (enough for each bowl of cut-up fruit, plus one spoon for each child)
- knife

Note: For each of the fruits being cut into chunks for this activity, be certain to have one more of that fruit that is not cut.

Procedure:

1. As the children observe you, select a fruit and cut it into small bite-sized pieces, and place them into a bowl.
2. Take the identical fruit that was not cut up, and place it adjacent to or behind the bowl that contains the cut-up fruit. For example, cut up an apple, place the chunks into a bowl, and place the extra apple (uncut) next to or behind the bowl. Be certain to put a clean spoon into each bowl of cut-up fruit.
3. Do this for all of the fruits that you have available for this activity.
4. Throughout this phase of the activity, use self-talk to narrate your actions. Talk about where the fruits come from and where they grow. Highlight the vibrant colors of each fruit.
5. Let the children taste each fruit as you complete cutting it up, identifying it as the children savor the piece.
6. When all of the fruits are cut up, have each child, by turn, close his/her eyes and open his/her mouth.

7. Select a fruit bit, and scoop it up with the spoon that is in the bowl. Transfer the fruit bit to the child's spoon, without touching the two spoons.
8. Place the fruit bit in the child's mouth.
9. Tell the child to open his/her eyes, chew the fruit, swallow, and guess which fruit it was.
10. Repeat this a few times for each child. It is quite funny when a child gets the bit of lemon!!!

Small Talk Suggestions:
Pre-Activity

- With all of the fruits visible to the children, say/ask:
  - "Watch me slice/cut up the _____." (Vocabulary Development; Commentary, Questioning, Requesting)
  - "I am slicing the fruit." (Present Progressive Tense)
  - "Who will help me slice the fruits?" (Questions [asking and/or responding]; Future Tense [will])
  - "Where do you think each fruit comes from?" (Questions [asking and/or responding]; Cognitive Skills)
- Draw the children's attention to the vibrant colors of the fruits.
  - "Who can find the red (yellow, green, orange, etc.) fruit for me to cut?" (Questions [asking and/or responding]; Auxiliary Verbs; Concept Development)
  - "Who drinks orange juice at home?" (Questions [asking and/or responding]; Present Tense Verbs)
  - "I do not like apple juice." (Negation)

During the Activity

- As the children take turns guessing which fruits they are tasting, ask:
  - "Would you like to taste the fruit?" (Questions [asking and/or responding]; Modals)
  - "Is it sweet (sour, bitter, salty, bland)?" (Questions [asking and/or responding]; Concept Development)

Post-Activity

- At Discussion or Circle Time:
  - "Did you enjoy our tasty guessing game?" (Questions [asking and/or responding]; Past Tense Verbs)

- "Which fruit did you enjoy the most?" (Questions [asking and/or responding]; Past Tense Verbs)

- Encourage the children to tell another child or adult how to play the game. (Pragmatics)
- Put one of the uncut fruit that was used in the game into a bag. Ask a child to put his/her hand into the bag and guess what the fruit is. Give each child a turn with a different fruit.
  - "Is it smooth (long, bumpy, rough, hot, cold)?" (Questions [asking and/or responding]; Concept Development; Vocabulary Review)
  - Play a game of "What Is Missing?" Using the fruits from the Tasty Guessing Game, place two fruits on the table before the children. Instruct one child to close his/her eyes. Take away one fruit, then direct the child to now open his/her eyes.
  - "What fruit is missing?" (Questions [asking and/or responding]; Concept Development; Cognitive Skills; Vocabulary Review)

- Stimulate a discussion about the various food groups (dairy, meats, vegetables, fruits). Name a food, and ask the children to takes turns expressing what food group the item belongs in. (Concept Development; Cognitive Skills; Vocabulary Review)

Suggestions

- Plan a trip to an orchard where fruit is grown. Arrange for the children to have an opportunity to actually pick fruits for themselves, especially a fruit that was included in the Tasty Guessing Game activity.
- Where possible, use the leftover fruit from the activity to make a fruit salad for everyone to enjoy as a snack or for dessert after lunch.
- A word of caution is warranted here. In several of the "Small Talk Suggestions," there are questions that the adult can use to stimulate a conversation with the child. Please do not feel compelled to "pepper" or bombard the child with question after question in order to establish and maintain a conversation. Rather, use one or two questions to get things started, but rely more upon commenting on what the child is doing, using grammatically intact sentences. In so doing, the adult is able to provide meaningful vocabulary that matches exactly what the child is engaged in at any given point during the activity.

ICE-CREAM SUNDAE ANY DAY!

Figure 3.2.   Ice-Cream Sundae Any Day.

√	COMMUNICATION SKILL	√	COMMUNICATION SKILL
√	Auxiliary Verbs		Pragmatics
√	Cognitive Skills	√	Present Progressive Tense
	Commentary, Questioning, Requesting	√	Present Tense Verbs
√	Concept Development	√	Requesting Assistance
√	Future Tense (will)	√	Questions (asking and/or responding)
√	Giving and Following Verbal Directives	√	Sequencing Skills
√	Modals	√	Vocabulary Development
√	Negation	√	Vocabulary Review
√	Past Tense Verbs		

Time Needed for Activity: Approximately 45 minutes to 1 hour
Difficulty Level: #1
Suggested Concepts and Vocabulary:

- sundae
- walnut
- syrup
- cherries
- ice cream
- jar
- container
- scoop

- vanilla
- chocolate
- top

Materials:

- 1-gallon container vanilla ice cream, or more depending upon the number of participants
- chocolate syrup (warmed)
- whipped cream topping, such as Reddi Whip
- 1 jar of chopped walnuts
- 1 jar of maraschino cherries
- ice-cream scoop(s) or spoons for each participant
- ice-cream sundae glasses or bowls for each participant

Procedure:

Direct the children to watch and listen as the teacher makes a sundae, verbalizing (self-talk) each action simultaneously. (Vocabulary Development)

1. Put a scoop of vanilla ice cream in an ice-cream sundae glass/bowl.
2. Pour about 2 ounces of warmed chocolate syrup on top of the vanilla ice cream.
3. Spoon 1 tablespoon of walnuts on top of the chocolate syrup.
4. Put some whipped cream atop the ice cream and nuts.
5. Crown with a cherry on top of the whipped cream.

Small Talk Suggestions:
Pre-Activity

- As the teacher is gathering the children together for the activity, say/ask:
  - "Who likes ice cream?" (Questions [asking and/or responding]; Present Tense Verbs)
  - "I bet _____ loves to eat ice cream." (Present Tense Verbs)
  - "What ingredients do we have here?" (Questions [asking and/or responding]; Vocabulary Development)

During the Activity

- As the teacher is helping the children perform the steps of the activity, ask/say:
  - "Who can/will scoop the ice cream?" (Questions [asking and/or responding]; Auxiliary Verbs; Modals; Future Tense [will])

- ○ "Who likes walnuts?" (Questions [asking and/or responding]; Present Tense Verbs)
- ○ "_____ is pouring the walnuts." (Present Progressive Tense; Vocabulary Development)

- As a child is doing the scooping of ice cream, ask the class:

  - ○ "Who is scooping the ice cream in the bowl/glass?" (Questions [asking and/or responding]; Present Progressive Tense)
  - ○ "Let's put a cherry on top!" (Concept Development)
  - ○ "_____ does not want a cherry." (Negation)

Post-Activity

- Upon completion of this activity, stimulate a discussion by using the following questions/comments:

  - ○ "Who enjoyed the ice-cream sundae?" "Why?" or "Why not?" (Questions [asking and/or responding]; Past Tense Verbs)
  - ○ "What ingredients did we need to make our ice-cream sundae?" (Cognitive Skills; Questions [asking and/or responding])
  - ○ "Why did we put the ice cream back in the freezer?" (Cognitive Skills; Questions [asking and/or responding])
  - ○ "Did the ice cream feel hot or cold?" (Questions [asking and/or responding]; Concept Development)
  - ○ "Did the syrup feel warm or cool?" (Questions [asking and/or responding]; Concept Development)
  - ○ "What other foods are served hot (cold, warm, cool)?" (Questions [asking and/or responding]; Concept Development)
  - ○ "What will happen to ice cream if we do not put it back into the freezer?" (Question [asking and/or responding]; Negation)

- Print the words "sundae" and "Sunday" on the board. Say the two words for the class.

  - ○ "Who can tell me how these two words are the same (different)?" (Questions [asking and/or responding]; Auxiliary Verbs; Modals)

- Days or weeks after performing this activity, lay out all of the equipment and ingredients for making an ice-cream sundae for the class to see. Encourage the children to be the teacher and to tell you how to make the sundae.

  - ○ "First you need the _____, then you have to _____." (Giving and Following Verbal Directives; Sequencing Skills; Vocabulary Review)

○ "What did we do last?" (Questions [asking and/or responding]; Concept Development)

• Put all of the sundae ingredients and equipment on a table, leaving out an essential ingredient or tool, such as ice cream or the sundae glass, etc. Wait for a child to verbalize or otherwise indicate that there is a problem. Then help the children figure out what the solution is. (Requesting Assistance)

Suggestions

• Ask the children to imagine other toppings they might want to try on their sundaes, such as M&Ms, coconut flakes, etc.
• Ask the children for their opinions of other topping ideas to try: jelly beans, spinach, chocolate sprinkles, carrots, peanuts, peanut butter, broccoli, honey, cookie crumbs, hot sauce, etc.

YUMMY BANANA SPLIT

Figure 3.3. Yummy Banana Split.

√	COMMUNICATION SKILL	√	COMMUNICATION SKILL
	Auxiliary Verbs		Pragmatics
√	Cognitive Skills	√	Present Progressive Tense
	Commentary, Questioning, Requesting	√	Present Tense Verbs
√	Concept Development	√	Requesting Assistance
	Future Tense (will)	√	Questions (asking and/or responding)
√	Giving and Following Verbal Directives	√	Sequencing Skills
	Modals	√	Vocabulary Development
√	Negation	√	Vocabulary Review
	Past Tense Verbs		

Time Needed for Activity: Approximately 45 minutes to 1 hour
Difficulty Level: #1
Suggested Concepts and Vocabulary:

- Nouns

  ○ strawberry, banana, tablespoon, teaspoon, bowl, scoop, whipped cream

- Action Words

  ○ pour, scoop, peel, slice

- Adjectives

  ○ vanilla, chocolate, strawberry, crushed/cubed

Materials:

- 1 container vanilla ice cream (enough for all participants)
- 1 container of chocolate ice cream (enough for all participants)
- 1 container strawberry ice cream (enough for all participants)
- 1 bunch of bananas (one for each participant)
- chocolate syrup
- fresh strawberries or strawberry ice-cream topping with sweetened syrup
- a can of crushed pineapple or pineapple chunks
- walnut ice-cream topping with syrup
- whipped cream
- maraschino cherries (with or without stems)
- ice-cream scoop or spoons for each child
- banana boats or bowls for each participant

Procedure:

1. Use the ice-cream scoop to place a scoop of each flavor of ice cream into each bowl.
2. The scoops of ice cream should be lined up adjacent to one another in a banana boat dish.
3. Peel the banana; cut about ¼ inch off both ends of the banana.
4. Slice the banana lengthwise, and place each half along the sides of the ice-cream row, pressing down a bit into the dish to keep the slices in place.
5. Pour 2 tablespoons of crushed pineapple or chucks on the vanilla ice cream, with an equal amount of chocolate syrup on the chocolate ice cream and strawberry topping on the strawberry ice cream.
6. Pour about a teaspoon of walnut topping over each scoop of ice cream.
7. Crown each scoop of ice cream with whipped cream, and top each scoop with a cherry.

Small Talk Suggestions:
Pre-Activity

- Place all of the materials on a table for the children to see.
  - "What did I bring in today?" (Questions [asking and/or responding]; Vocabulary Development)
  - "Who knows what we are going to make?" (Questions [asking and/or responding]; Cognitive Skills; Vocabulary Development)
  - "Where do pineapples come from?" (Questions [asking and/or responding]; Cognitive Skills; Vocabulary Development)

During the Activity

- As the activity progresses, ask/say:

    ○ "Who likes bananas?" (Questions [asking and/or responding]; Present Tense Verbs; Vocabulary Development)

    ○ "_____, please peel the bananas." (Requesting Assistance)

    ○ "Who is cutting the banana?" (Questions [asking and/or responding]; Present Progressive Tense; Vocabulary Development)

    ○ "_____ does not like cherries (or other fruit)." (Negation; Vocabulary Development)

    ○ "Who is scooping the ice cream?" (Present Progressive Tense; Vocabulary Development)

    ○ "I bet _____ wants more ice cream!" (Present Tense Verbs; Vocabulary Development)

    ○ "What colors do you see in our banana boats?" (Concept Development; Vocabulary Development)

    ○ "What do you think ice cream is made from?" (Questions [asking and/or responding]; Vocabulary Development)

    ○ "Where does milk come from?" (Questions [asking and/or responding]; Vocabulary Development)

Post-Activity

- As the children prepare to eat their banana splits, instruct one child to be the monitor in charge of giving out the utensils.

    ○ "Ask _____ to give you a spoon (bowl, napkin, etc.)." (Questions [asking and/or responding]; Vocabulary Development; Vocabulary Review)

- Invite another teacher or other adult to the classroom, and offer him/her a banana split. Have one of the children be in charge of explaining to another child how to make the banana split for the guest.

    ○ "_____, tell _____ what to do first, second, and third." (Giving and Following Verbal Directives; Sequencing Skills; Vocabulary Review)

    ○ "I think I will make a banana split for _____. _____, please tell me step-by-step how to make a banana split." (Giving and Following Verbal Directives; Sequencing Skills; Vocabulary Review)

- A few days or weeks after all have had fun making banana splits, try the activity again; but this time, "forget" to put out a key ingredient, such as the bananas. Tell the children to start making their banana splits, and wait to see if they communicate their need. (Requesting Assistance; Vocabulary Review)

Suggestion

Get the children to help make a banana snack. Depending upon how many participants will be involved, get two or three bananas and slice them, widthwise, into approximately 1-inch pieces. Spread some peanut butter on the top of each piece, then dip the peanut butter side into some crunchy granola. Try adding a raisin or a blueberry or both. Enjoy!!!

MAKING AN ICE-CREAM FLOAT

Figure 3.4.   Making an Ice-Cream Float.

√	COMMUNICATION SKILL	√	COMMUNICATION SKILL
	Auxiliary Verbs		Pragmatics
	Cognitive Skills	√	Present Progressive Tense
√	Commentary, Questioning, Requesting	√	Present Tense Verbs
	Concept Development		Requesting Assistance
	Future Tense (will)	√	Questions (asking and/or responding)
√	Giving and Following Verbal Directives	√	Sequencing Skills
	Modals	√	Vocabulary Development
	Negation	√	Vocabulary Review
√	Past Tense Verbs		

Time Needed for Activity: Approximately 40 minutes to 1 hour
Difficulty Level: #1
Suggested Concepts and Vocabulary:

- soda pop
- ice cream
- straw
- glass
- flavor
- ice-cream float
- spoons
- pour
- tall

- long
- sweet

Materials:

- ice cream (a variety of flavors)
- soda (a cola will do just fine)
- tall glass for each child
- long straw for each child

Procedure:

1. Drop a scoop of ice cream into the glass.
2. Pour soda slowly over the ice cream, all the way to the top.
3. Grab a straw, and enjoy!

Small Talk Suggestions:
Pre-Activity

- Describe the activity to the children, explaining what an ice-cream float is and telling them about the utensils and ingredients needed. Make sure that all items are somewhere in the area and in plain sight.

    ◦ "Who likes ice cream?" (Present Tense Verbs; Questions [asking and/or responding]; Vocabulary Development)
    ◦ "Who sees the ice cream/spoons/soda/napkins?" (Questions [asking and/or responding]; Present Tense Verbs)
    ◦ "Who enjoys soda?" (Questions [asking and/or responding]; Present Tense Verbs)
    ◦ Who wants to enjoy ice cream and soda together?" (Questions [asking and/or responding]; Present Tense Verbs)

- Name each activity item, instructing different children to go get items named by the teacher.

    ◦ "_____, please get the spoons/glasses/napkins." (Vocabulary Development)

During the Activity

- Involve the children in the making of their individual ice-cream floats.

    ◦ "Who is scooping the ice cream?" (Questions [asking and/or responding]; Present Progressive Tense)

- ○ "Scoop the ice into the tall glasses." (Commentary, Questioning, Requesting; Giving and Following Verbal Directives)
- ○ "_____ is pouring the soda." (Present Progressive Tense)
- ○ "Is the soda sweet enough?" (Questions [asking and/or responding]

Post-Activity

- Display the equipment and ingredients used for the ice-cream float activity. Hold up or point to each item as you say/ask:

    - ○ "What is this?" (Questions [asking and/or responding]; Vocabulary Review)
    - ○ "We made ice-cream floats." (Past Tense Verbs)
    - ○ "How did we make our ice-cream floats?" (Questions [asking and/or responding]; Sequencing Skills)
    - ○ What ice-cream flavor did you like/dislike?" (Questions [asking and responding])
    - ○ "_____ loves sweet treats." (Present Tense Verbs)

Suggestion

Here is another ice-cream idea. Core a few apples, then slice them, widthwise. Each participant will need two slices of apple. To keep the slices from turning brown, place the apple slices in a bowl and toss them in about a tablespoon of lemon juice. Next, place a small scoop of ice cream on one apple slice, then top with the second slice. If several of these apple ice-cream sandwiches must be made, store each completed sandwich in a freezer until they are ready to serve.

MAKING A SALAD

Figure 3.5. Making a Salad.

√	COMMUNICATION SKILL	√	COMMUNICATION SKILL
	Auxiliary Verbs		Pragmatics
	Cognitive Skills	√	Present Progressive Tense
√	Commentary, Questioning, Requesting	√	Present Tense Verbs
√	Concept Development		Requesting Assistance
√	Future Tense (will)	√	Questions (asking and/or responding)
	Giving and Following Verbal Directives	√	Sequencing Skills
	Modals	√	Vocabulary Development
√	Negation	√	Vocabulary Review
√	Past Tense Verbs		

Time Needed for Activity: Approximately 40 to 50 minutes
Difficulty Level: #1
Suggested Concepts and Vocabulary:

- lettuce
- carrots
- yellow bell pepper
- red bell pepper
- cucumber
- tomatoes
- vegetables
- croutons

- toss
- sprinkle
- slice
- healthy/unhealthy
- color words associated with the ingredients

Materials:

- 1 each of the following: tomato, carrot, yellow bell pepper, red bell, pepper, green bell pepper, cucumber
- bag of prewashed romaine lettuce or raw spinach
- croutons
- roasted almonds
- salad dressing (have several flavors available for the children to choose from)
- large mixing bowl
- sharp knife
- cutting board

Procedure:

1. Pour some of the lettuce or spinach into the large mixing bowl.
2. Rinse the tomato, carrot, peppers, cucumber, and any other vegetables chosen for the salad.
3. Cut up the vegetables and drop them into the bowl.
4. Pour about a cup of croutons and a cup of roasted almonds over the vegetables, and toss.
5. Dish the salad into individual bowls.
6. Top each bowl of salad with the desired dressing.

Small Talk Suggestions:
Pre-Activity

- Lay out all of the fresh vegetables and other utensils needed to make the salad, naming each one as you go.

  - "Can you guess what we are going to make?" (Questions [asking and/or responding])
  - "Who can tell me what this is (point to each item, one at a time)?" (Questions [asking and/or responding]; Vocabulary Development)
  - "Who will help me cut up the vegetables?" (Questions [asking and/or responding]; Future Tense [will])

During the Activity

- Engage the children in each aspect of making the salad.
  - "_____ loves carrots. Right?" (Present Tense Verbs)
  - "_____ does not/doesn't like vegetables." (Negation)
  - "_____ is slicing the carrots." (Present Progressive Tense; Vocabulary Development)
  - "What colors are in our salads?" (Concept Development; Vocabulary Development; Questions [asking and/or responding])

Post-Activity

- Discuss the activity either later during Circle Time or while the children are eating their salads.
  - "Who made salad today?" (Past Tense Verbs; Questions [asking and/or responding]; Vocabulary Review)
  - "How did we make the salad?" (Sequencing Skills; Vocabulary Review)
  - "Why should we eat salad?" (Questions [asking and/or responding]; Vocabulary Development; Vocabulary Review)
  - "What does the word 'healthy' mean?" (Questions [asking and responding]; Vocabulary Development)
  - "Tell me why eating only candy every day is not healthy/is unhealthy." (Commentary, Questioning, Requesting; Vocabulary Development; Vocabulary Review)

Suggestion

Think about the salad item that the children seem to enjoy the most, lettuce, radishes, carrots, whatever; then obtain the seeds for that vegetable. Locate a plot of soil on the school's campus where a small vegetable garden could be planted with the assistance of the children. Together, plant the seeds, weed the garden, harvest the vegetables, then prepare a nutritious salad.

ICE-CREAM WAFFLES

Figure 3.6.   Ice-Cream Waffles.

√	COMMUNICATION SKILL	√	COMMUNICATION SKILL
	Auxiliary Verbs		Pragmatics
√	Cognitive Skills	√	Present Progressive Tense
√	Commentary, Questioning, Requesting		Present Tense Verbs
√	Concept Development		Requesting Assistance
√	Future Tense (will)	√	Questions (asking and/or responding)
√	Giving and Following Verbal Directives	√	Sequencing Skills
	Modals	√	Vocabulary Development
	Negation	√	Vocabulary Review
√	Past Tense Verbs		

Time Needed for Activity: Approximately 40 minutes to 1 hour
Difficulty Level: #1
Suggested Concepts and Vocabulary:

- waffles
- strawberries
- bananas
- syrup
- fruit cocktail
- toast
- slice
- drizzle

Materials:

- packages of frozen waffles, enough for each child to make at least one waffle dessert
- a variety of flavors of ice cream (enough for each child to have one scoop)
- sliced strawberries
- sliced bananas
- chocolate syrup
- whipped cream topping
- can of fruit cocktail
- toaster

Procedure:

1. Put waffles into the toaster, and toast to the desired amount.
2. Place one waffle on a plate.
3. Place a scoop of ice cream onto the waffle.
4. Spoon 1 to 2 tablespoons of strawberries and bananas and/or fruit cocktail on top of the ice cream.
5. Drizzle some chocolate syrup over the ice cream and fruits.
6. Place about 2 tablespoons or more of whipped cream on top, and sprinkle more fruit, to taste.
7. Enjoy!!!

Small Talk Suggestions:
Pre-Activity

- Tell the children what they will be creating. Place the equipment, ingredients, and utensils in the snack area or the kitchen area of the classroom within reach of the children.
  - "What do we need to make our tasty dessert snack?" (Questions [asking and/or responding]; Vocabulary Development; Cognitive Skills)
  - "_____, please get the (activity item)." Permit different children to retrieve different items for the activity. (Vocabulary Development; Giving and Following Verbal Directives)
  - "What do we need to toast our frozen waffles?" (Questions [asking and/or responding]; Cognitive Skills; Vocabulary Development)

During the Activity

- Involve the children in the preparation of the waffles.
  - "Who will help me toast the waffles?" (Questions [asking and/or responding]; Future Tense [will])

- ○ "_____ is toasting the waffles for us." (Present Progressive Tense)
- ○ "_____ toasted/warmed the waffles." (Past Tense Verbs)
- ○ "Let's scoop some ice cream onto the waffles." (Giving and Following Verbal Directives)
- ○ "_____ is spooning some fruits on his/her waffle." (Present Progressive Tense)
- ○ "Are waffles the same as pancakes?" (Questions [asking and/or responding]; Vocabulary Development)
- ○ "What shapes can you see in our waffles?" (Concept Development; Vocabulary Development; Cognitive Skills; Questions [asking and/or responding])
- ○ "Watch me drizzle some chocolate syrup on top of the ice cream." (Commentary, Questioning, Requesting)

Post-Activity

- Try taking photos of the children as they participate in the dessert preparation. Three to four photos may be enough. Instruct the children to put the photos in the correct order.

  - ○ "What did we do first, second, third?" (Sequencing Skills; Vocabulary Review)

Suggestion

Instead of using only one waffle for the ice-cream snack, place some tasty ice cream between two waffles for a waffle ice-cream sandwich.

MAKING TRAIL MIX

Figure 3.7.   Making Trail Mix.

√	COMMUNICATION SKILL	√	COMMUNICATION SKILL
	Auxiliary Verbs		Pragmatics
√	Cognitive Skills	√	Present Progressive Tense
	Commentary, Questioning, Requesting	√	Present Tense Verbs
√	Concept Development		Requesting Assistance
√	Future Tense (will)	√	Questions (asking and/or responding)
√	Giving and Following Verbal Directives	√	Sequencing Skills
	Modals	√	Vocabulary Development
	Negation	√	Vocabulary Review
√	Past Tense Verbs		

Time Needed for Activity: Approximately 30 to 40 minutes
Difficulty Level: #1
Suggested Concepts and Vocabulary:

- sunflower seeds
- almonds
- peanuts
- raisins (plain, yogurt-covered)
- dried pineapple
- dried banana
- dried apple
- sweetened coconut flakes

- M&Ms (optional)
- pour
- stir

Materials:

- shelled sunflower seeds, toasted almonds, peanuts, raisins, dried fruits (pineapple, banana, apple, etc.), enough for each child to have about ½ cup
- flaked coconut (enough for each child to have about ¼ cup)
- large bowl
- large lidded container
- large salad spoon
- ziplock sandwich bags for each child

Procedure:

1. Pour all of the ingredients into the large bowl.
2. Stir the ingredients together until they are well distributed.
3. Spoon some of the mixture into individual ziplock bags to enjoy at snack time.
4. Store the rest in the large lidded container.

Small Talk Suggestions:
Pre-Activity

- Place each container of ingredients beside a large bowl on a table in front of the children.

  - "Who can guess what we will do with these ingredients?" (Future Tense [will]; Cognitive Skills; Vocabulary Development; Questions [asking and/or responding])
  - "We are going to make something called trail mix. Does anyone know how to make trail mix?" (Cognitive Skills; Vocabulary Development)
  - "What goes into our trail mix?" (Questions [asking and/or responding]; Vocabulary Development)

During the Activity

- Involve the children in making this light snack.

  - "Let's pour the raisins/nuts/coconut flakes/dried fruits, etc., into the large bowl." (Giving and Following Verbal Directives; Vocabulary Development)

- ○ "Who wants to pour the ingredients into the large bowl?" (Present Tense Verbs; Questions [asking and/or responding])
- ○ "Who will mix our ingredients?" (Questions [asking and/or responding]; Future Tense [will])
- ○ "_____ is mixing our trail mix." (Present Progressive Tense)
- ○ "_____ is pouring the _____." (Present Progressive Tense)

Post-Activity

- Discuss the trail mix activity during Circle Time.

  - ○ "How did we make our trail mix? What did we use?" (Vocabulary Review; Sequencing Skills)
  - ○ "_____ stirred the trail mix." (Past Tense Verbs)
  - ○ "How did the trail mix taste?" (Past Tense Verbs; Concept Development; Questions [asking and/or responding])

Suggestion

Plan a Children's Film/Video Festival with carefully selected videos that the children will enjoy. Before the showing, prepare a snack of trail mix to be eaten during the video(s). Invite another class, and either make the trail mix for the guests or teach them how to make the scrumptious snack. Encourage the children who already know how to make the snack to teach the guests how to make the trail mix.

FRUITY YOGURT PARFAIT

Figure 3.8.   Fruity Yogurt Parfait.

√	COMMUNICATION SKILL	√	COMMUNICATION SKILL
	Auxiliary Verbs		Pragmatics
√	Cognitive Skills	√	Present Progressive Tense
√	Commentary, Questioning, Requesting		Present Tense Verbs
	Concept Development		Requesting Assistance
√	Future Tense (will)	√	Questions (asking and/or responding)
√	Giving and Following Verbal Directives	√	Sequencing Skills
√	Modals	√	Vocabulary Development
√	Negation	√	Vocabulary Review
√	Past Tense Verbs		

Time Needed for Activity: Approximately 40 to 50 minutes
Difficulty Level: #1
Suggested Concepts and Vocabulary:

- yogurt
- strawberries
- bananas
- granola
- slices
- tablespoons
- teaspoons
- parfait
- spoon

Materials:

- strawberries and bananas, sliced (or any other fruits desired), enough for each child to have about ½ cup
- large container of plain or vanilla yogurt (children might prefer the flavor of vanilla)
- large container of granola
- parfait glasses or any other tall glass for each participant
- spoons for each ingredient

Procedure:

1. Place a few slices of banana on the bottom of each glass.
2. Put about two tablespoons of yogurt on the banana.
3. Add layers of the rest of the ingredients in any way desired. Let the children be as creative as they like!
4. Have fun!!!

Small Talk Suggestions:
Pre-Activity

- Gather the activity materials as the children observe.

  - "Can someone tell me what you think we'll do with these things?" (Questions [asking and/or responding]; Cognitive Skills; Future Tense [will])
  - "We will make a yogurt parfait." (Future Tense [will])

- Hold up each ingredient and utensil.

  - "Tell me what this is." (Vocabulary Development)

During the Activity

- Get the children involved by saying/asking:

  - "Who will help me spoon the yogurt/slices of bananas/slices of strawberries into the glass?" (Future Tense [will])
  - "Who is sprinkling granola on top of the yogurt?" (Present Progressive Tense)
  - "Can you spoon the fruit into my glass?" (Modals)
  - "_____ sprinkled granola on his/her yogurt." (Past Tense Verbs)
  - "This is called a yogurt parfait!" (Commentary, Questioning, Requesting)
  - "_____ does not like yogurt." (Negation)

Post-Activity

- Ask the children to tell you how to make a fruity parfait for someone, and follow their directions.

  ○ "What did we make today?" (Past Tense Verbs)
  ○ "_____, tell me how to make a fruity parfait." (Giving and Following Verbal Directives; Vocabulary Review)

- Ask the children to explain in sequence what they did to make the fruity parfaits.

  ○ "What did we spoon first?" (Sequencing Skills)
  ○ "What did we do next?" (Sequencing Skills)

Suggestion

Encourage the child to help the adult solve a problem. For example, as the adult puzzles over a small problem, she/he might ask the child for an idea to solve the issue or an opinion about a possible solution. For example, if the teacher is planning to rearrange furniture in the classroom, she/he might ask the child for ideas as to where certain pieces should be placed.

MAKING JELL-O

Figure 3.9. Making Jello-O.

√	COMMUNICATION SKILL	√	COMMUNICATION SKILL
√	Auxiliary Verbs		Pragmatics
√	Cognitive Skills	√	Present Progressive Tense
√	Commentary, Questioning, Requesting	√	Present Tense Verbs
√	Concept Development		Requesting Assistance
√	Future Tense (will)	√	Questions (asking and/or responding)
√	Giving and Following Verbal Directives	√	Sequencing Skills
√	Modals	√	Vocabulary Development
√	Negation	√	Vocabulary Review
√	Past Tense Verbs		

Time Needed for Activity: This project will need to begin on one day, then continue over to the next day for the Jell-O to gel for eating.

Difficulty Level: #1

Suggested Concepts and Vocabulary:

- fruit cocktail (including the specific names of fruits found in the fruit cocktail)
- combine
- stir
- chill
- pour
- boiling
- hot
- cold

Materials: (double or triple the ingredients to accommodate the number of participants in the activity)

- one 6-ounce package of Jell-O (any flavor will suffice)
- 2 cups of boiling water
- 2 cups of cold water
- 1½ to 3 cups of well-drained fruits, such as fruit cocktail
- large bowl

Procedure:

1. In a large bowl, combine the Jell-O and the boiling water.
2. Stir the mixture until the gelatin is completely dissolved.
3. Stir the cold water into the mixture.
4. Place the bowl of Jell-O in the refrigerator, and let it chill for 1½ hours. The mixture needs to thicken a bit.
5. Into the thickened Jell-O, stir in the fruit.
6. Place the bowl of fruit Jell-O into the refrigerator for 4 hours, so it becomes firm.
7. Enjoy this tasty treat!

Small Talk Suggestions:
Pre-Activity

- Explain to the children what the activity will be, and ask them to use a shopping basket to walk around the room and collect all the supplies needed to make the Jell-O dessert. Be certain that all equipment and ingredients are somewhere in the classroom.

  ○ "How do we make Jell-O?" (Questions [asking and/or responding]; Sequencing Skills; Vocabulary Development)
  ○ "Who eats Jell-O at home?" (Questions [asking and/or responding]; Present Tense Verbs; Vocabulary Development)
  ○ "Go shopping around the classroom for everything we will need to make our Jell-O." (Giving and Following Verbal Directives; Future Tense [will]; Vocabulary Development)

During the Activity

- Perform/Direct the activity while using self-talk and parallel talk.

  ○ "Do you like Jell-O?" (Auxiliary Verbs; Questions [asking and/or responding])
  ○ "Who can open the box of Jell-O?" (Auxiliary Verbs; Modals)

- ○ "_____ likes (specific Jell-O flavor)." (Present Tense Verbs)
- ○ "I do not like (Jell-O flavor)." (Negation)
- ○ "I will pour the hot water." (Future Tense [will])
- ○ "Watch me combine the water and the Jell-O." (Giving and Following Verbal Directives)
- ○ "Watch me mix the water with the Jell-O." (Giving and Following Verbal Directives)
- ○ "Who is pouring the cold water?" (Questions [asking and/or responding]; Present Progressive Tense)
- ○ "Who is stirring the Jell-O into the water?" (Present Progressive Tense)
- ○ "What is happening to the Jell-O powder?" (Questions [asking and/or responding]; Cognitive Skills)

- Once the Jell-O is firm and ready to eat, put one child in charge of giving out the utensils.

  - ○ "Please ask _____ to give you a bowl/napkin/spoon/etc." (Questions [asking and/or responding])

Post-Activity

- After the Jell-O has been eaten, ask:

  - ○ "Who liked the Jell-O flavor?" (Questions [asking and/or responding]; Past Tense Verbs)
  - ○ "Remember how only I poured the hot water? Why wouldn't I let you pour the hot water?" (Commentary, Questioning, Requesting; Cognitive Skills; Concept Development; Vocabulary Review)
  - ○ What Jell-O flavor should we try next time?" (Questions [asking and/or responding]; Vocabulary Review)

Suggestion

Find a way to reach out to parents and other caretakers in the children's lives, and emphasize the importance of reading aloud to their youngsters at least once a day. A nighttime story is an ideal way to end a day and a perfect way to facilitate the development of age-appropriate language skills.

CHAPTER 3

SOUP TIME!

Figure 3.10. Soup Time!

√	COMMUNICATION SKILL	√	COMMUNICATION SKILL
	Auxiliary Verbs		Pragmatics
√	Cognitive Skills	√	Present Progressive Tense
	Commentary, Questioning, Requesting	√	Present Tense Verbs
√	Concept Development		Requesting Assistance
√	Future Tense (will)	√	Questions (asking and/or responding)
	Giving and Following Verbal Directives		Sequencing Skills
√	Modals	√	Vocabulary Development
√	Negation	√	Vocabulary Review
√	Past Tense Verbs		

Time Needed for Activity: Approximately 30 to 45 minutes
Difficulty Level: #1
Suggested Concepts and Vocabulary:

- sauce pan
- spoon
- napkin
- can
- soup
- can opener
- stir
- open
- letters of the alphabet

Materials:

- large saucepan
- large spoon
- cans of alphabet soup (enough for each child to enjoy a bowlful)
- can opener(s)
- small bowls, spoons, and napkins for students

Procedure:

1. Open the can(s) of soup.
2. Pour the contents into the saucepan.
3. Heat the soup, stirring occasionally.
4. When the soup is warm enough, ladle portions into the bowls for each student. (Be certain that a generous number of alphabet letters are in each child's bowl.)
5. Use the letters in the bowls to create words.
6. Try to use the letters to spell each child's name in his/her bowl.

Small Talk Suggestions:
Pre-Activity

- Display all of the equipment and ingredients for the activity.

  - "Who can tell me what we will be making today?" (Questions [asking and/or responding]; Future Tense [will])
  - "What do we have on our table today?" (Questions [asking and/or responding]; Vocabulary Development)
  - "Who can open the cans of soup?" (Modals) Or: "Who will open the cans of soup?" (Future Tense [will])
  - "Look at the label on the soup can. What kind of soup is this?" (Questions [asking and/or responding]; Cognitive Skills)

During the Activity

- Direct the children to perform different soup-making tasks. As the children help to prepare the soup snack, comment on what they are doing as they do it. In effect, narrate their actions:

  - "Who is opening the soup cans?" (Present Progressive Tense)
  - "_____ will give out the napkins." (Future Tense [will])
  - "_____ eats soup for lunch." (Present Tense Verbs)
  - "What are you doing, _____?" (Questions [asking and/or responding])

- Once the soup is ready, and the children are enjoying it, talk about the letters of the alphabet.

  ○ "Who has the letter 'A' in his/her soup?" (Questions [asking and/or responding]; Concept Development) Then ask the children to find various other letters in their soup.
  ○ "Can you find the first letter of your first name (last name) in your soup?" (Questions [asking and/or responding]; Modals)

Post-Activity

- Talk about the soup-making experience either at the snack table as the children finish their soup or during Circle Time to wrap up the day's activities.

  ○ "Who liked our soup today?" (Questions [asking and/or responding]; Past Tense Verbs; Vocabulary Review)
  ○ "Who did not like the soup? Why?" (Questions [asking and/or responding]; Negation; Vocabulary Review)
  ○ "Let's sing the Alphabet Song." (Concept Development; Vocabulary Review)
  ○ "What did we spell in our alphabet soup?" (Questions [asking and/or responding]; Vocabulary Review)

Suggestion

Obtain a bag of soup crackers, such as oyster crackers. For each child, drop a number of oyster crackers into her/his soup, and ask her/him to count how many oyster crackers are in the soup. Use a different number for each child.

MAKING A SANDWICH

Figure 3.11. Making a Sandwich.

√	COMMUNICATION SKILL	√	COMMUNICATION SKILL
	Auxiliary Verbs		Pragmatics
	Cognitive Skills		Present Progressive Tense
√	Commentary, Questioning, Requesting		Present Tense Verbs
	Concept Development	√	Requesting Assistance
√	Future Tense (will)	√	Questions (asking and/or responding)
√	Giving and Following Verbal Directives	√	Sequencing Skills
√	Modals	√	Vocabulary Development
	Negation	√	Vocabulary Review
√	Past Tense Verbs		

Time Needed for Activity: Approximately 40 minutes
Difficulty Level: #1
Suggested Concepts and Vocabulary:

- names of selected sandwich meats being used for the activity
- mayonnaise
- mustard
- lettuce
- tomatoes
- knife
- cut
- spread

Materials:

- loaf of sandwich bread (enough for all of the children)
- mayonnaise and/or mustard
- assorted sandwich meats
- a bag of prewashed lettuce
- tomatoes (sliced)
- plates
- napkins
- knife

Procedure:

1. Instruct the children to watch you carefully as you make your own sandwich.
2. Use the knife to spread mayonnaise or mustard on two slices of bread.
3. Lay some lettuce on the bread.
4. Continue adding sandwich ingredients to the rest of the sandwich until done.
5. Tell the children that it is now their turn to do what you did.
6. Then it is time to chow!

Small Talk Suggestions:
Pre-Activity

- Show the children all of the ingredients for the activity. Hold up each item, and say its name.

  - "Hmmm, I have slices of bread and mayonnaise/mustard. I have lunch meats, like ham, salami, chicken, turkey. What do you think we will make today?" (Questions [asking and/or responding]; Future Tense [will]; Vocabulary Development)
  - "Can you help me make sandwiches for our lunch?" (Modals)

During the Activity

- Hand out jars of mayonnaise and mustard to a few of the children, but be certain that the jars are too tightly closed for little hands to open.

  - "Open the jars, so we can start making our sandwiches." (Giving and Following Verbal Directives; Requesting Assistance) Watch/Listen for indications from the children that they need help in opening the jars. Try modeling requests for assistance by saying the following:

    * "I think (child's name) needs help. Say 'I need help.'"

- Encourage the children to direct the activity by telling the teacher how to make her/his sandwich.

  ○ "_____, please tell me how to make my sandwich. Tell me what to do." (Commenting, Questioning, Requesting; Sequencing Skills)

Post-Activity

- As the children finish their sandwiches, ask:

  ○ "Who finished his/her sandwich?" (Questions [asking and/or responding]; Past Tense Verbs)
  ○ "Who can tell me how to make a sandwich?" (Questions [asking and/or responding]; Sequencing Skills; Vocabulary Review)

Suggestion

Try as much as possible to be aware of all adults who interact with the children. It is imperative that each adult who works in the classroom show abundant interest in what the child is saying. The activities in this book are intended to generate oral communication. A child who is ignored or who feels that no one is listening will slowly decrease attempts at interacting with others. Even if it is difficult to understand the child's speech or language, express interest in what she/he is saying.

MAKING A SHIRLEY TEMPLE

Figure 3.12.   Making a Shirley Temple.

√	COMMUNICATION SKILL	√	COMMUNICATION SKILL
	Auxiliary Verbs	√	Pragmatics
	Cognitive Skills	√	Present Progressive Tense
	Commentary, Questioning, Requesting	√	Present Tense Verbs
√	Concept Development		Requesting Assistance
√	Future Tense (will)	√	Questions (asking and/or responding)
	Giving and Following Verbal Directives	√	Sequencing Skills
√	Modals	√	Vocabulary Development
	Negation	√	Vocabulary Review
√	Past Tense Verbs		

Time Needed for Activity: Approximately 40 minutes
Difficulty Level: #1
Suggested Concepts and Vocabulary:

- ice cubes
- soda
- lemon
- lime
- juice
- cherries
- fill
- divide

- stir
- crown
- color words associated with this beverage

Materials:

- ice cubes
- 3 cups of lemon-lime soda
- juice of one lime
- 4 teaspoons of grenadine
- maraschino cherries
- 4 glasses (Note: This recipe is for four servings. To serve more than four students, simply adjust the recipe to accommodate the appropriate number of students in the class.)

Procedure:

1. Fill each glass with ice cubes.
2. Divide the soda between the glasses.
3. Divide the lime juice between the glasses.
4. Stir a teaspoon of grenadine into each glass.
5. Crown each glass with a maraschino cherry.

Small Talk Suggestions:
Pre-Activity

- Place the utensils and ingredients in front of the children.

  - "Who knows what we are doing today?" (Questions [asking and/or responding]; Present Tense Verbs)
  - "Tell me what you see on the table." (Vocabulary Development)

During the Activity

- Engage the children in the making of their Shirley Temples.

  - "_____, would you please give out the glasses?" (Questions [asking and/or responding]; Modals)
  - "Who is putting ice cubes in the glasses?" (Questions [asking and/or responding]; Present Progressive Tense)
  - "_____, can you help me pour some soda?" (Questions [asking and/or responding]; Modals)

- ◦ "_____ is pouring some soda." (Questions [asking and/or responding]; Present Progressive Tense)
- ◦ "Who will pour some lime juice?" (Questions [asking and/or responding]; Future Tense [will])
- ◦ "What else do you think we need?" (Questions [asking and/or responding])
- ◦ "_____ is stirring the grenadine in the glasses." (Present Progressive Tense)
- ◦ "_____, can you put one cherry in each glass?" (Questions [asking and/or responding]; Modals; Concept Development)

Post-Activity

- • Invite someone to the classroom to tell that person what the children did to make their own Shirley Temples.

  - ◦ "I have an idea. Let's invite Ms./Mr. _____ to our classroom, so we can tell her/him what we made." (Vocabulary Review; Pragmatics; Sequencing Skills)
  - ◦ "_____ drank her/his Shirley Temple very slowly." (Past Tense Verbs)
  - ◦ "I stirred my Shirley Temple with a straw." (Past Tense Verbs)

Suggestion

While it is important to give the child attention when she/he is speaking, it is also important to get the child's attention before verbal directives are to be given. Adequate listening skills are vital to learning, in general.

BOWLING

Figure 3.13.   Bowling.

√	COMMUNICATION SKILL	√	COMMUNICATION SKILL
√	Auxiliary Verbs		Pragmatics
	Cognitive Skills	√	Present Progressive Tense
√	Commentary, Questioning, Requesting	√	Present Tense Verbs
√	Concept Development		Requesting Assistance
	Future Tense (will)	√	Questions (asking and/or responding)
√	Giving and Following Verbal Directives	√	Sequencing Skills
	Modals	√	Vocabulary Development
	Negation	√	Vocabulary Review
√	Past Tense Verbs		

Time Needed for Activity: Approximately 30 minutes
Difficulty Level: #1
Suggested Concepts and Vocabulary:

- cartons
- ball
- toss
- bowl
- rolling
- words for number concepts
- words for numeral identification
- taking turns

Materials:

- 10 quart-sized milk or juice cartons, empty, each numbered 1 through 10 (Print the numbers on a piece of paper, and paste a number on each carton.)
- a foam-rubber ball or a Nerf ball

Procedure:

1. With your child assisting you, set up the cartons in the same way that bowling pins are set for a game.
2. Stand a few feet back from the cartons, and draw a line or use some other marking to show where the players must stand.
3. Take turns tossing or rolling the ball toward the cartons to see who can knock down the most cartons on two tries.
4. Help your child count how many cartons were knocked down and/or how many cartons were left standing.

Note: If you are using milk cartons, you may wish to use this opportunity to talk about where milk comes from. This could lead to a discussion of how other farm animals help people by providing food.

Small Talk Suggestions:
Pre-Activity

- Place markings on the floor to designate where each carton should be placed.

  - "Hey, everyone! Let's go bowling in the classroom! Take one of the cartons, and place each one on a mark that I put on the floor." (Giving and Following Verbal Directives; Vocabulary Development)
  - "_____, what number do you have?" (Questions [asking and/or responding]; Concept Development; Vocabulary Development)

During the Activity

- Explain to the children how to bowl. Designate who will be first, second, third, and so forth.

  - "May I go first?" (Questions [asking and/or responding]; Concept Development)
  - "Okay! Who bowls first?" (Questions [asking and/or responding]; Concept Development; Present Tense Verbs)
  - "_____ is rolling the ball!" (Present Progressive Tense)

- ○ "What is the number on the carton(s) that you knocked down?" (Questions [asking and/or responding]; Concept Development)
- ○ "How many cartons do you think you will knock down?" (Questions [asking and/or responding])

- After some cartons are knocked down, ask:

  - ○ "How many cartons were knocked down?" (Questions [asking and/or responding]; Concept Development)
  - ○ "How many cartons are still standing?" (Questions [asking and/or responding]; Concept Development)

Post-Activity

- As the activity wraps up, ask:

  - ○ "Did you have fun bowling?" (Questions [asking and/or responding]; Past Tense Verbs)
  - ○ "What did you like about bowling?" (Questions [asking and/or responding]; Commentary, Questioning, Requesting)
  - ○ "Who knocked down the most cartons?" (Questions [asking and/or responding]; Concept Development)
  - ○ "Who remembers how we set up our bowling activity? Tell me how." (Questions [asking and/or responding]; Sequencing Skills; Vocabulary Review)
  - ○ "Do you like bowling?" (Questions [asking and/or responding]; Auxiliary Verbs)
  - ○ "What other games can you play with a ball?" (Concept Development; Vocabulary Development; Questions [asking and/or responding])

Suggestion

Try placing some or all of the milk carton bowling pins on a table, and instruct the children, in turn, to toss a ball to see how many bowling pins they can knock down. Have the children check the numerals printed on the bowling pins, and tell the class which pins they hit with the ball and/or identify the pins that were not knocked down.

RECORDING SESSION

Figure 3.14.   Recording Session.

√	COMMUNICATION SKILL	√	COMMUNICATION SKILL
√	Auxiliary Verbs		Pragmatics
√	Cognitive Skills	√	Present Progressive Tense
√	Commentary, Questioning, Requesting	√	Present Tense Verbs
	Concept Development		Requesting Assistance
√	Future Tense (will)	√	Questions (asking and/or responding)
√	Giving and Following Verbal Directives	√	Sequencing Skills
√	Modals	√	Vocabulary Development
	Negation	√	Vocabulary Review
√	Past Tense Verbs		

Time Needed for Activity: Approximately 20 to 30 minutes
Difficulty Level: #1
Suggested Concepts and Vocabulary:

- record
- rehearse
- practice
- sing
- song

Materials:

- cassette tape recorder or another recording device, such as a digital recorder
- blank cassette

Procedure:

1. Talk with the children about their favorite songs. Sing the songs together. You might even teach them a few songs that you remember from your childhood.
2. Make a tape recording of the children singing a few songs.

Small Talk Suggestions:
Pre-Activity

- Talk with the children about the songs sung in the classroom. Make a list of the songs.
  - "What are some of your favorite songs?" (Questions [asking and/or responding]; Commentary, Questioning, Requesting)
- Show the children the recording equipment.
  - "What did I bring in today?" (Questions [asking and/or responding]; Vocabulary Development)
  - "Can you guess what we are going to do today?" (Questions [asking and/or responding]; Cognitive Skills; Modals)

During the Activity

- Suggest that the children rehearse/practice the songs to be recorded.
  - "What songs will we record?" (Questions [asking and/or responding]; Future Tense [will])
  - "Let's rehearse the songs that we will record." (Vocabulary Development)
  - "Let's practice the songs that we will record." (Vocabulary Development)
  - "_____ loves to sing this song." (Present Tense Verbs)
  - "We are singing nicely together." (Present Progressive Tense)
- After the rehearsals have been completed, announce to the children that it is time to record.
  - "Okay. I think we are ready to record our songs. Are you ready?" (Questions [asking and/or responding]; Commentary, Questioning, Requesting)

- Record all songs agreed upon.

  ○ "Okay, everyone. Let's record our songs!" (Giving and Following Verbal Directives)

Post-Activity

- Have a discussion after the recording session has been completed.

  ○ "Do you think we did a good job?" (Questions [asking and/or responding]; Auxiliary Verbs; Past Tense Verbs)
  ○ "Let's listen to our recording." (Giving and Following Verbal Directives)
  ○ "All of you sang very nicely!" (Commentary, Questioning, Requesting; Past Tense Verbs)
  ○ "_____ loves to sing." (Present Tense Verbs)
  ○ "Help me think of what to do with our recording." (Requesting Assistance)
  ○ "Let's put the cassette in an envelope with decorations on it, like stickers and glitter. What do you think?" (Questions [asking and/or responding]; Commentary, Questioning, Requesting)
  ○ "I have another idea, too! Let's put our recording in the Listening Center or class library. What do you think of that idea?" (Questions [asking and/or responding]; Commentary, Questioning, Requesting)
  ○ "Let's tell _____ what we did today!" (Sequencing Skills; Vocabulary Development; Vocabulary Review)

Suggestion

Encourage each of the children to sing a solo verse of some of the songs recorded. Permit a child to sing a song entirely on her/his own. Where possible, ask the district's media center or some other service to make multiple copies of the audio tape/CD to distribute to each child for home. Maybe there is a teacher or other support person who knows how to make CD copies on a computer.

WHICH ONE IS MISSING?

√	COMMUNICATION SKILL	√	COMMUNICATION SKILL
√	Auxiliary Verbs		Pragmatics
√	Cognitive Skills		Present Progressive Tense
	Commentary, Questioning, Requesting		Present Tense Verbs
	Concept Development		Requesting Assistance
	Future Tense (will)	√	Questions (asking and/or responding)
√	Giving and Following Verbal Directives	√	Sequencing Skills
	Modals	√	Vocabulary Development
	Negation	√	Vocabulary Review
	Past Tense Verbs		

Time Needed for Activity: Approximately 15 to 20 minutes
Difficulty Level: #1
Suggested Concepts and Vocabulary:

- words pertaining to items selected by the teacher

Materials:

- 5 to 10 common classroom/household items that the children are likely to be familiar with, such as a bar of soap, a toothbrush, a pencil, a cup and a spoon, an eraser, chalk, a crayon, a blank book, a pen, construction paper, a paintbrush, a tempera paint bottle, etc.

Procedure:

1. Place each of the selected items on a table in full view of the children.
2. Take some time to name each item, and talk about its function in the classroom and within the classroom setting.
3. Select a child to be "It."
4. As all of the children carefully watch, choose 3 (or just 2 initially) of the items, and place them side-by-side.
5. Instruct the "It" child to close his/her eyes.
6. Remove one of the items.
7. Tell the child to open his/her eyes and guess which item is missing.
8. Let each child have 2 or 3 chances, correct or incorrect; then let the next child be "It," until all have had an opportunity to play. Change the items for each guessing attempt as desired.

Small Talk Suggestions:
Pre-Activity

- Bring all of the selected items to the table.

  ◦ "Look at everything that I found for today." (Giving and Following Verbal Directives)
  ◦ "What is this?" (Questions [asking and/or responding]; Vocabulary Development)
  ◦ "What does this do?" (Questions [asking and/or responding]; Auxiliary Verbs; Cognitive Skills; Vocabulary Development)
  ◦ "Do you have one at home?" (Questions [asking and/or responding]; Auxiliary Verbs)

During the Activity

- Choose a child to be "It," and select 2 or 3 of the items discussed. Place them in front of the selected child.

  ◦ "Okay, _____. Close your eyes!" (Giving and Following Verbal Directives)
  ◦ "Keep them closed." (Giving and Following Verbal Directives)
  ◦ "Open your eyes!" (Giving and Following Verbal Directives)
  ◦ "Guess which one is missing!" (Questions [asking and/or responding])
  ◦ "Do you know which one is missing?" (Questions [asking and/or responding]; Auxiliary Verbs)

Post-Activity

- At some point later in the day, give each child an opportunity to play "Teacher" while an adult plays the part of a student. Instruct the "Teacher" to select 2 or 3 items from the aforementioned item pool and place the items in front of the "Student," saying the name of each item.

  ◦ "Put the items down in front of Ms./Mr. _____." (Giving and Following Verbal Directives; Vocabulary Review)
  ◦ "Tell Ms./Mr. _____ what to do next." (Sequencing Skills; Giving and Following Verbal Directives)

- Continue the activity until each child has had a chance to be the "Teacher."

Suggestion

Where appropriate, do not forget the language development value of using self-talk during all classroom activities, such art activities, field trips, science projects, etc. This does not mean endless talking about what the teacher is doing, but rather uttering a meaningful comment about her/his actions as an activity is progressing. Sparingly narrate one's actions.

SOUNDS GUESSING GAME

√	COMMUNICATION SKILL	√	COMMUNICATION SKILL
√	Auxiliary Verbs		Pragmatics
√	Cognitive Skills	√	Present Progressive Tense
√	Commentary, Questioning, Requesting		Present Tense Verbs
	Concept Development		Requesting Assistance
√	Future Tense (will)	√	Questions (asking and/or responding)
√	Giving and Following Verbal Directives		Sequencing Skills
√	Modals	√	Vocabulary Development
	Negation	√	Vocabulary Review
√	Past Tense Verbs		

Time Needed for Activity: Approximately 15 to 20 minutes
Difficulty Level: #1
Suggested Concepts and Vocabulary:

- words pertaining to the selected sound sources

Materials:

- a tape recorder
- a blank cassette
- sound sources

Procedure:

1. Take some time to go about the classroom/school building and a home, recording a variety of sounds associated with those environments. The sounds might include a pencil sharpener, a photocopy machine, the PA system, children playing in the school yard, a bouncing basketball in the gym, a flushing toilet, running water, pages being turned in a book, a vacuum cleaner, a blender, a ticking clock, the ringing of an alarm clock, the sounding of a smoke detector, an electric razor, the telephone, etc. Try to have as many environmental sounds as possible for the sake of variety. Be sure to have a brief pause between each sound.
2. Sit with the children and play back the sounds, one at a time.
3. Encourage the children to listen carefully then identify each sound that is heard.

Small Talk Suggestions:
Pre-Activity

- Explain to the children the importance of being good listeners.

  ◦ "What do we listen with?" (Questions [asking and/or responding]; Vocabulary Development; Auxiliary Verbs)
  ◦ "Why is good listening important for all of us?" (Questions [asking and/or responding]; Commentary, Questioning, Requesting)
  ◦ "What sounds do you like to hear?" (Questions [asking and/or responding]; Commentary, Questioning, Requesting)

During the Activity

- Explain to the children that each will get a chance to listen to a sound played by the teacher. The child must guess what he/she hears.

  ◦ "Listen to this sound." (Cognitive Skills; Giving and Following Verbal Directives)
  ◦ "What is that?" (Questions [asking and/or responding])
  ◦ "_____ is listening." (Present Progressive Tense)
  ◦ "_____ is guessing." (Present Progressive Tense)
  ◦ "Can you guess what sound you hear?" (Questions [asking and/or responding]; Modals)
  ◦ "Will _____ guess correctly?" (Questions [asking and/or responding]; Future Tense [will])

Post-Activity

- After all of the children have had an opportunity to guess a few sounds, have a discussion.

  ◦ "Who remembers the sounds that we heard?" (Questions [asking and/or responding]; Past Tense Verbs; Vocabulary Review)

Suggestion

Record different people (10 or so) in the school building whom the children are familiar with. Instruct each person (child or adult) to say a predetermined sentence that is long enough for the listener to get an adequate sampling of the speaker's voice. Next, play one sentence, and ask the children to guess who the speaker is.

1-2-3 RED LIGHT

√	COMMUNICATION SKILL	√	COMMUNICATION SKILL
√	Auxiliary Verbs		Pragmatics
	Cognitive Skills	√	Present Progressive Tense
	Commentary, Questioning, Requesting	√	Present Tense Verbs
	Concept Development		Requesting Assistance
√	Future Tense (will)	√	Questions (asking and/or responding)
√	Giving and Following Verbal Directives	√	Sequencing Skills
√	Modals		Vocabulary Development
	Negation	√	Vocabulary Review
√	Past Tense Verbs		

Time Needed for Activity: Approximately 30 minutes
Difficulty Level: #1
Suggested Concepts and Vocabulary:

- traffic cop
- police officer
- traffic light

Materials: None

Procedure:

1. This game is best played with four or more children.
2. Start by selecting one child to be the "Traffic Cop." His/Her job will be to call out "1-2-3 Red light!" or "Green light!"
3. Instruct the other children to go to the starting line about 16 feet from where the Traffic Cop stands, at the finish line.
4. Now, tell the Traffic Cop to turn away from the other children, so he/she cannot see them. When ready, the Traffic Cop should shout, "Green light!" At this second, the children should quickly run toward the finish line near the Traffic Cop.
5. After just a few seconds, the Traffic Cop should shout, "1-2-3 Red light," and immediately turn around.
6. When the other children hear "Red light," they must quickly stop running toward the finish line.
7. If the Traffic Cop catches anyone still moving, he/she will send that child back to the starting line. The first child to reach the finish line is the winner.

Small Talk Suggestions:
Pre-Activity

- As the children gather together, explain how 1-2-3 Red Light is played.

    ○ "Did you ever play Red Light?" (Questions [asking and/or responding]; Auxiliary Verbs)
    ○ "Who will be the Traffic Cop?" (Questions [asking and/or responding]; Future Tense [will])
    ○ "The Traffic Cop turns around and hides his/her eyes. Next, he/she shouts, 'Green light,' and everyone starts to run toward the finish line. Next, the Traffic Cop shouts, '1-2-3 Red light!' as he/she turns around to see you." (Sequencing Skills; Giving and Following Verbal Directives)
    ○ "When the Traffic Cop shouts, 'Red Light,' everyone must stop running to the finish line. If the Traffic Cop catches anyone still moving, he/she can make you go back to the start line. The first person to get to the finish line without getting caught by the Traffic Cop is the winner. The winner gets to be the next Traffic Cop." (Giving and Following Verbal Directives)

During the Activity

- Where appropriate, say:

    ○ "_____ is hiding his/her eyes!" (Present Progressive Tense)
    ○ "The cars are moving." (Present Progressive Tense)
    ○ "The car stops!" (Present Tense Verbs)
    ○ "The cars stopped!" (Past Tense Verbs)
    ○ "The car goes." (Present Tense Verbs)

Post-Activity

- Discussion Time/Circle Time might go something like this:

    ○ "Who won our 1-2-3 Red Light game?" (Questions [asking and/or responding]; Past Tense Verbs)
    ○ "What does a real Traffic Cop do?" (Questions [asking and/or responding]; Modals)
    ○ "Who knows another name for 'cop'?" (Questions [asking and/or responding])
    ○ "What does the red traffic light mean?" (Questions [asking and/or responding]; Vocabulary Review)
    ○ "What does the green light mean?" (Questions [asking and/or responding]; Vocabulary Review)

Suggestion

Tell the class about childhood games that used to be played but are rarely observed among children today, such as Duck, Duck, Go, Simon Says, Marco Polo, Hide-and-Seek, etc. Select a game, and teach it to the children.

CLAY TIME!

Figure 3.15.   Clay Time!

√	COMMUNICATION SKILL	√	COMMUNICATION SKILL
	Auxiliary Verbs	√	Pragmatics
	Cognitive Skills	√	Present Progressive Tense
	Commentary, Questioning, Requesting	√	Present Tense Verbs
√	Concept Development		Requesting Assistance
√	Future Tense (will)	√	Questions (asking and/or responding)
√	Giving and Following Verbal Directives	√	Sequencing Skills
√	Modals	√	Vocabulary Development
	Negation	√	Vocabulary Review
√	Past Tense Verbs		

Time Needed for Activity: Approximately 30 to 45 minutes
Difficulty Level: #1
Suggested Concepts and Vocabulary:

- salt
- flour
- water
- plastic bag
- words associated with selected food coloring

Materials:

- ½ cup of salt
- 2 cups of flour
- ¾ cup of water
- plastic bags
- food coloring
- bowl

Procedure:

1. Pour the flour and salt into a bowl.
2. Mix these ingredients together until they are blended well.
3. Slowly, add no more than ¾ of a cup of water to this mixture until it becomes smooth and thick like modeling clay.
4. If you like, add a few drops of food coloring.
5. Have fun with your child, making shapes and animals from the homemade clay.
6. Use the plastic bags to store the clay in the refrigerator.

Small Talk Suggestions:
Pre-Activity

- Tell the children what the planned activity is, but they must go around the room, retrieving the needed supplies.

  ◦ "Would you please get the _____?" (Vocabulary Development; Giving and Following Verbal Directives; Modals; Questions [asking and/or responding])

During the Activity

- Engage the children in making their own clay.

  ◦ "What will we do with the _____?" (Future Tense [will]; Questions [asking and/or responding])
  ◦ "_____ is pouring the _____." (Present Progressive Tense)
  ◦ "_____ pours the _____." (Present Tense Verbs)
  ◦ "Help me measure the _____." (Giving and Following Verbal Directives)

- Once the modeling clay has been made, ask:

  ◦ "Let's make some shapes! Who can make a circle?" (Concept Development; Giving and Following Verbal Directives)
  ◦ "Can you help me make some letters of the alphabet?" (Modals; Questions [asking and/or responding])

Post-Activity

- As the class is cleaning up, hold up different items from the activity:

  - "What is this?" (Vocabulary Review; Questions [asking and/or responding])
  - "So, what did we make today?" (Vocabulary Review; Questions [asking and/or responding])
  - "We made our own clay!" (Past Tense Verbs)
  - "_____ rolled the clay into a ball." (Past Tense Verbs)
  - "I pounded my clay into a pancake!" (Past Tense Verbs)

- Invite an adult to stop by the classroom, so the children can have an opportunity to talk about their experience.

  - "Tell _____ what we did today." (Pragmatics)
  - "What did we have to do first, then second, and then next?" (Sequencing Skills; Vocabulary Review; Questions [asking and/or responding])

Suggestion

Permit the children to make modeling clay and create their own sculptures. Give each sculpture a chance to dry and harden, then display each work of art in the class library. Invite guests to visit the art gallery.

KNICKKNACK BOX

Figure 3.16.   Knickknack Box.

√	COMMUNICATION SKILL	√	COMMUNICATION SKILL
√	Auxiliary Verbs		Pragmatics
√	Cognitive Skills	√	Present Progressive Tense
√	Commentary, Questioning, Requesting	√	Present Tense Verbs
√	Concept Development	√	Requesting Assistance
√	Future Tense (will)	√	Questions (asking and/or responding)
√	Giving and Following Verbal Directives		Sequencing Skills
	Modals	√	Vocabulary Development
	Negation	√	Vocabulary Review
√	Past Tense Verbs		

Time Needed for Activity: Approximately 45 minutes to 1 hour
Difficulty Level: #1
Suggested Concepts and Vocabulary:

- the names of shapes, such as "circle," "square," "triangle," "rectangle"
- any other shape names used for this activity

Materials:

- an empty shoe box with the lid
- colored construction paper precut into 1- to 2-inch geometric shapes, such as circles, squares, triangles, rectangles, and any other shapes desired (The pictured example in figure 3.16 used precut hearts.)

- stickers
- Elmer's glue

Procedure:

1. Work with the child to cover the entire shoe box and its lid with the colored shapes, using the glue.
2. Add a few stickers, if desired.
3. Set the box aside until the glue has dried completely.
4. When completed, the child will have a special place to put crayons, pencils, etc., in a neat spot.

Small Talk Suggestions:
Pre-Activity

- Show the children a completed knickknack box. Let them also see the box's interior with some of the teacher's odds and ends in it.

  ○ "I made a knickknack box to keep my pens and pencils and erasers in a neat spot." (Past Tense Verbs; Commentary, Questioning, Requesting; Vocabulary Development)
  ○ "Would you like to make a knickknack box, also?" (Questions [asking and/or responding])
  ○ "What will you keep in your box?" (Future Tense [will]; Questions [asking and/or responding])
  ○ "What supplies will we need to make our boxes?" (Questions [asking and/or responding]; Future Tense [will]; Vocabulary Development)

- Put one of the children in charge of getting out the materials needed for the activity.

  ○ "Ask _____ for all of the supplies you need." (Requesting Assistance; Vocabulary Development; Giving and Following Verbal Directives; Cognitive Skills)

During the Activity

- Comment on the children's work as they progress through the activity.

  ○ "_____ is selecting different shapes for his/her box." (Vocabulary Development; Present Progressive Tense)
  ○ "_____ likes circles/squares/triangles/rectangles for his/her box." (Present Tense Verbs; Concept Development)
  ○ "_____, what shape are you gluing to your box?" (Questions [asking and/or responding]; Concept Development)

- ○ "The circle is my favorite shape." (Concept Development; Vocabulary Development)
- ○ "What is your favorite shape?" (Concept Development; Vocabulary Development; Questions [asking and/or responding])

Post-Activity

- • Discussion/Circle Time may go something like this:

  - ○ "Did we make a knickknack box today?" (Auxiliary Verbs; Questions [asking and/or responding]; Vocabulary Review)
  - ○ "How many circles/squares/triangles/rectangles are glued on your box?" (Questions [asking and/or responding]; Concept Development; Past Tense Verbs; Vocabulary Review)

Suggestion

Where appropriate, do not forget the language development value of using parallel talk during all classroom activities, such art activities, field trips, science projects, etc. This does not mean endless talking about what the child is doing, but rather uttering a meaningful comment about her/his actions as an activity is progressing. Sparingly narrate the actions of the child during an activity.

MAKE A TRAFFIC LIGHT

Figure 3.17.   Make a Traffic Light.

√	COMMUNICATION SKILL	√	COMMUNICATION SKILL
√	Auxiliary Verbs		Pragmatics
√	Cognitive Skills	√	Present Progressive Tense
√	Commentary, Questioning, Requesting		Present Tense Verbs
√	Concept Development		Requesting Assistance
	Future Tense (will)	√	Questions (asking and/or responding)
	Giving and Following Verbal Directives		Sequencing Skills
√	Modals	√	Vocabulary Development
	Negation	√	Vocabulary Review
	Past Tense Verbs		

Time Needed for Activity: Approximately 20 to 30 minutes
Difficulty Level: #1
Suggested Concepts and Vocabulary:

- traffic
- traffic light
- safe

Materials:

- one empty shoe box that has been spray-painted black for each child
- construction paper (red, yellow, green)
- Elmer's glue

Procedure:

1. Help each child cut out an appropriately sized (in relation to the size of the shoe box) red circle, yellow circle, and green circle.
2. Stand the shoe box vertically, and glue the green circle to the bottom spot, the yellow circle to the middle position, and the red circle at the top.

Small Talk Suggestions:
Pre-Activity

- Have a completed traffic light ready while talking with the children about traffic safety.

  ○ "When is it safe to cross the street?" (Questions [asking and/or responding]; Cognitive Skills; Vocabulary Development)
  ○ "What is a traffic light?" (Questions [asking and/or responding]; Commentary, Questioning, Requesting; Vocabulary Development)
  ○ "Do you see colors on the traffic light?" (Questions [asking and/or responding]; Concept Development; Auxiliary Verbs; Vocabulary Development)
  ○ "What colors are on the traffic light?" (Questions [asking and/or responding]; Concept Development; Vocabulary Development)
  ○ "Who knows what the green light/red light/yellow light means?" (Questions [asking and/or responding]; Concept Development; Cognitive Skills; Vocabulary Development)
  ○ "Let's make traffic lights! What do we need?" (Commentary, Questioning, Requesting)

During the Activity

- Draw attention to what the children are doing as they are doing it.

  ○ "_____ is cutting out circles for the traffic lights." (Present Progressive Tense)
  ○ "What colors will your traffic lights be?" (Questions [asking and/or responding]; Concept Development)
  ○ "How many colors will you have on your traffic light?" (Questions [asking and/or responding]; Concept Development)

Post-Activity

- Discussion/Circle Time

  ○ "What did we make today?" (Questions [asking and/or responding]; Vocabulary Review)

- ○ "What is the shape of our traffic light?" (Questions [asking and/or responding]; Vocabulary Review; Cognitive Skills; Concept Development)
- ○ "What are the shapes of the lights?" (Questions [asking and/or responding]; Vocabulary Review; Cognitive Skills; Concept Development)
- ○ "Should we cross the street when the traffic light is red for us?" (Questions [asking and/or responding]; Vocabulary Review; Cognitive Skills; Concept Development; Modals)
- ○ "When is it safe to cross the street?" (Questions [asking and/or responding]; Vocabulary Review; Cognitive Skills; Concept Development)

Suggestion

Use short but grammatically correct sentences when speaking with the child.

PAPER PLATE PIZZA

Figure 3.18. Paper Plate Pizza.

√	COMMUNICATION SKILL	√	COMMUNICATION SKILL
	Auxiliary Verbs		Pragmatics
	Cognitive Skills	√	Present Progressive Tense
	Commentary, Questioning, Requesting	√	Present Tense Verbs
√	Concept Development		Requesting Assistance
√	Future Tense (will)	√	Questions (asking and/or responding)
√	Giving and Following Verbal Directives		Sequencing Skills
√	Modals	√	Vocabulary Development
√	Negation	√	Vocabulary Review
√	Past Tense Verbs		

Time Needed for Activity: Approximately 30 to 45 minutes
Difficulty Level: #1
Suggested Concepts and Vocabulary:

- pizza
- deliver
- slice
- circle
- rectangle
- triangle
- prefer

Materials:

- paper plate for each participant
- red crayons
- brown construction paper cut into circles about the size of half-dollars
- green construction paper cut into circles about the size of quarters
- yellow construction paper cut into rectangles about ½ by 1 inch in size

Procedure:

1. Each participant gets one paper plate.
2. Use the red crayon to color the paper plate red. That will be the tomato sauce.
3. When the children are ready, instruct them to select a few yellow rectangles (cheese) to paste to the pizza.
4. Next, instruct the children to use some of the brown circles (sausages) to paste to the pizza.
5. Have the children take a few of the green circles. Show them how to use the red crayon to make a dot in the middle of the circle. The green circle is the olive, and the red dot is the pimento.
6. Instruct the children to paste the olives anywhere they choose on their pizza.

Small Talk Suggestions:
Pre-Activity

- Show the children examples of paper plate pizzas made by the teacher.
  - "Who likes to eat pizza?" (Questions [asking and/or responding]; Vocabulary Development)
  - "Did you ever eat pizza for lunch or for dinner?" (Questions [asking and/or responding]; Vocabulary Development)
  - "Is pizza a good food for breakfast?" (Questions [asking and/or responding]; Vocabulary Development)
  - "Does pizza taste better when it's hot or cold?" (Questions [asking and/or responding]; Vocabulary Development)
  - "_____ ate pizza yesterday." (Vocabulary Development; Past Tense Verbs)
  - "When I went bowling with my friends, we ate pizza." (Vocabulary Development; Questions [asking and/or responding]; Past Tense Verbs)
  - "I made pizza at home for a party." (Past Tense Verbs)

- As the children view the teacher's completed pizzas, ask:
  - "Now, what supplies do you think you will need for your pizzas?" (Questions [asking and/or responding]; Future Tense [will]; Vocabulary Development)
  - "Ask _____ to get the supplies for you." (Vocabulary Development)

During the Activity

- Make a paper plate pizza along with the children to provide a model for them.
  - "Let's color the paper plate with our red crayons." (Giving and Following Verbal Directives)
  - "What color is the tomato sauce on a pizza?" (Questions [asking and/or responding]; Vocabulary Development; Concept Development)
  - "We're using brown circles for the sausage." (Present Progressive Tense; Vocabulary Development)
  - "We cannot eat our paper plate pizzas. Right?" (Negation; Questions [asking and/or responding])
  - "Who eats sausage on their pizza?" (Questions [asking and/or responding]; Present Tense Verbs)
  - "I know _____ likes to eat olives." (Present Tense Verbs)
  - "_____ enjoys cheese." (Present Tense Verbs)
  - "I do not like lots of cheese." (Negation)
  - "_____ loves pieces of chicken on her pizza!" (Present Tense Verbs)
  - "When we finish making our paper plate pizzas, we can't eat these pizzas. No way!" (Negation)
  - "_____ is coloring the pizza red." (Present Progressive Tense)
  - "Who are you making your pizza for, _____?" (Questions [asking and/or responding]; Vocabulary Development)
  - "Will your pizza be for a birthday party, dinner, or some other special occasion?" (Questions [asking and/or responding]; Future Tense [will]; Vocabulary Development)
  - "Would you like to make another paper plate pizza with different toppings?" (Questions [asking and/or responding]; Modals)

Post-Activity

- Discussion/Circle Time
  - "What is your favorite pizza topping, _____?" (Questions [asking and/or responding]; Vocabulary Development)

- ○ "Do you prefer green olives or black olives?" (Questions [asking and/or responding]; Vocabulary Development)
- ○ "Would you like to make another paper plate pizza with only cheese on it?" (Questions [asking and/or responding]; Modals; Vocabulary Development)

• Holding up each item used in the activity, ask:

- ○ "What is this?" (Questions [asking and/or responding; Vocabulary Review)
- ○ "What did we use this for?" (Questions [asking and/or responding]; Vocabulary Review)

Suggestion

Plan a real class pizza party, and invite another class as guests. Make a paper plate pizza to attach the invitation to.

PERSONAL PHOTO ALBUM

√	COMMUNICATION SKILL	√	COMMUNICATION SKILL
√	Auxiliary Verbs		Pragmatics
√	Cognitive Skills	√	Present Progressive Tense
	Commentary, Questioning, Requesting	√	Present Tense Verbs
√	Concept Development	√	Requesting Assistance
√	Future Tense (will)	√	Questions (asking and/or responding)
	Giving and Following Verbal Directives		Sequencing Skills
	Modals	√	Vocabulary Development
	Negation	√	Vocabulary Review
√	Past Tense Verbs		

Time Needed for Activity: Approximately 30 to 40 minutes
Difficulty Level: #1
Suggested Concepts and Vocabulary:

- camera
- paper fastener
- words for parts of face

Materials:

- a digital camera
- a digital picture printer
- sheets of construction paper
- paper fasteners

Procedure:

1. Photograph each child as he/she performs different activities in the classroom or throughout the school. Be certain to have one portrait-style shot of the child as the front page of each photo album. Funny faces are encouraged!!
2. Have fun watching the printer print out the photographs.
3. Fasten one photo to each sheet of construction paper, then attach a paper fastener to the upper left-hand corner of the new photo album.

Small Talk Suggestions:
Pre-Activity

- Show the children a photo album of the teacher. Let them see members of the family, the teacher as a child of the same age as the children viewing the photos, etc.

  ○ "What did I bring in today?" (Questions [asking and/or responding]; Vocabulary Development)
  ○ "Do you want to make a photo album?" (Questions [asking and/or responding]; Auxiliary Verbs)
  ○ "Tell me what we will need to make our photo albums." (Vocabulary Development; Cognitive Skills; Future Tense [will])

During the Activity

- Permit the children to decide where they want their photos taken as they engage in a variety of actions.

  ○ "_____ is posing for the camera." (Vocabulary Development; Present Progressive Tense)
  ○ "_____ poses so nicely for the camera!" (Present Tense Verbs)

- Print the photos for all of the children, and distribute them to the children. Permit them to arrange the photos in the order they desire.

  ○ "Which photo do you want first, second, third, fourth, and fifth?" (Questions [asking and/or responding]; Concept Development; Vocabulary Development)
  ○ "_____ is gluing his/her photos to the construction paper." (Present Progressive Tense; Vocabulary Development)
  ○ "Let me know if you need help using the paper fasteners." (Requesting Assistance; Vocabulary Development)

Post-Activity

- Arrange the completed photo albums in a gallery along the walls of the classroom or outside the classroom. Wherever the gallery is placed, let that area be used for the Discussion/Circle Time area.

  ○ "What did we do today?" (Questions [asking and/or responding]; Vocabulary Development; Vocabulary Review)

- Stop in front of each photo album and ask:

  ○ "Who is this?" (Questions [asking and/or responding])
  ○ "Is this a boy or a girl?" (Questions [asking and/or responding])

- "What color is his/her hair?" (Questions [asking and/or responding]; Concept Development)
- "What color are his/her eyes?" (Questions [asking and/or responding]; Concept Development)
- "How many eyes do you have?" (Questions [asking and/or responding]; Concept Development)
- "How many noses do you have?" (Questions [asking and/or responding]; Concept Development)
- "How many ears do you have?" (Questions [asking and/or responding]; Concept Development)
- "I like how you posed in this picture." (Vocabulary Development; Past Tense Verbs)

Suggestion

Plan a fun event where each child brings in a very young baby picture of herself/himself. Display the pictures side-by-side on a wall, then give the children some time to see if they can tell which classmate is depicted in each photo. For more fun, see if other teachers that the children know would bring in their own baby pictures for this event.

FEEL IT

√	COMMUNICATION SKILL	√	COMMUNICATION SKILL
	Auxiliary Verbs	√	Pragmatics
√	Cognitive Skills	√	Present Progressive Tense
√	Commentary, Questioning, Requesting		Present Tense Verbs
√	Concept Development		Requesting Assistance
√	Future Tense (will)	√	Questions (asking and/or responding)
√	Giving and Following Verbal Directives	√	Sequencing Skills
√	Modals	√	Vocabulary Development
	Negation	√	Vocabulary Review
	Past Tense Verbs		

Time Needed for Activity: Approximately 15 to 20 minutes
Difficulty Level: #1
Suggested Concepts and Vocabulary:

- words associated with selected objects to be placed in the box
- smooth
- bumpy
- rough
- hard
- soft

Materials:

- a "Feel It" box
- objects of varying textures, small enough to fit in the box

Procedure:

1. Create a Feel It box by selecting a box, such as a large shoe box (maybe for boots).
2. Cut a hole in the end of the box that is large enough for a child to fit his/her hand through.
3. Place an object in the box without letting the children see it.
4. Direct a child to reach through the hole to feel the object placed within.
5. The child must describe how the object feels, using descriptors, such as hard, soft, bumpy, smooth, sharp, rough, etc.
6. Ask the child to identify the object!

Small Talk Suggestions:
Pre-Activity

- Show the children the Feel It box. Point out the hole at its end, and tell why it is there.
  - "Can you guess what we are going to do with the Feel It box?" (Modals; Vocabulary Development; Questions [asking and/or responding])

During the Activity

- Put a preselected object into the box and say/ask:
  - "Close your eyes while I put something into the box." (Giving and Following Verbal Directives)
  - "_____, put your hand in the Feel It box." (Giving and Following Verbal Directives)
  - "Tell me how it feels." (Giving and Following Verbal Directives; Concept Development; Cognitive Skills)
  - "What will _____ feel in the box? (Future Tense [will]; Questions [asking and/or responding])
  - "_____ is feeling the object." (Present Progressive Tense)
  - "Think of a word to describe what it feels like." (Concept Development; Vocabulary Development; Giving and Following Verbal Directives)
  - "Is it bumpy or smooth?" (Concept Development; Vocabulary Development; Questions [asking and/or responding])
  - "Is it hard or soft?" (Concept Development; Vocabulary Development; Cognitive Skills; Questions [asking and/or responding])
  - "Guess what it is!" (Giving and Following Verbal Directives; Vocabulary Development)

Post-Activity

- Talk about different objects and words associated with their textures.
  - "Different things feel differently." (Commentary, Questioning, Requesting)
  - "Is a handkerchief hard or soft?" (Questions [asking and/or responding]; Concept Development; Vocabulary Review)
  - "Is a pencil sharp or dull?" (Questions [asking and/or responding]; Concept Development; Vocabulary Review)
  - "Is sandpaper rough or smooth?" (Questions [asking and/or responding]; Concept Development; Vocabulary Review)

- ○ "A handkerchief is not hard." (Commentary, Questioning, Requesting; Concept Development; Vocabulary Review)
- ○ "A pencil is not dull." (Commentary, Questioning, Requesting; Concept Development; Vocabulary Review)
- ○ "Sandpaper is not smooth." (Commentary, Questioning, Requesting; Concept Development; Vocabulary Review)
- ○ "Let's tell _____ what we did today." (Pragmatics; Sequencing Skills)

Suggestion

Permit some of the children to select objects to place in the Feel It box, so the teacher gets a chance to guess.

HAPPY OR SAD?

√	COMMUNICATION SKILL	√	COMMUNICATION SKILL
√	Auxiliary Verbs		Pragmatics
√	Cognitive Skills	√	Present Progressive Tense
√	Commentary, Questioning, Requesting		Present Tense Verbs
√	Concept Development		Requesting Assistance
√	Future Tense (will)	√	Questions (asking and/or responding)
√	Giving and Following Verbal Directives	√	Sequencing Skills
√	Modals	√	Vocabulary Development
√	Negation	√	Vocabulary Review
√	Past Tense Verbs		

Time Needed for Activity: Approximately 15 to 20 minutes
Difficulty Level: #1
Suggested Concepts and Vocabulary:

- happy
- sad

Materials:

- magazine cutouts of people with various facial expressions

Procedure:

1. Spread the pictures out on the table, face-down.
2. Each child takes a turn selecting a picture to turn over.
3. The child must determine whether the pictured individual is happy or sad, then make up a reason why the person feels that way.

Small Talk Suggestions:
Pre-Activity

- Instruct the children to help the teacher spread the pictures on the table, face-down.
  - "Take some of these pictures, and help me spread them all over the table, face-down." (Giving and Following Verbal Directives)
  - "_____ is helping me spread out the pictures." (Present Progressive Tense)
  - "The person's face must be down, not up." (Concept Development; Giving and Following Verbal Directives)

- Explain to the children how the game will proceed.

  ○ "We will take turns." (Future Tense [will]; Giving and Following Verbal Directives)
  ○ "I will go first." (Concept Development; Giving and Following Verbal Directives)

During the Activity

- Model the activity by going first. Encourage the children to make up a reason about why the person in the selected picture is happy or sad.

  ○ "Okay, I am picking a picture, like this one!" (Present Progressive Tense)
  ○ "I have a picture of a boy." (Commentary, Questioning, Requesting)
  ○ "The boy has a happy face." (Concept Development; Vocabulary Development; Commentary, Questioning, Requesting)
  ○ "The boy is not sad." (Concept Development; Vocabulary Development)
  ○ "Hmmm! I think he is happy because today is his birthday!" (Commentary, Questioning, Requesting)
  ○ "Can you guess why the man is sad?" (Modals; Questions [asking and/or responding])
  ○ "_____, now it is your turn!" (Sequencing Skills)
  ○ "_____ is looking for a picture to select." (Present Progressive Tense)
  ○ "_____ selected a picture!" (Past Tense Verbs)
  ○ "_____ cannot decide what picture to select." (Negation)

Post-Activity

- Discussion/Circle Time

  ○ "What makes you feel happy?" (Questions [asking and/or responding]; Concept Development; Vocabulary Review)
  ○ "What makes you feel sad?" (Questions [asking and/or responding]; Concept Development; Vocabulary Review)
  ○ "What do you do when you feel sad?" (Cognitive Skills; Concept Development; Vocabulary Review)
  ○ "Do you ever feel angry about something?" (Auxiliary Verbs; Cognitive Skills; Questions [asking and/or responding]; Vocabulary Review)
  ○ "What made you angry?" (Commentary, Questioning, Requesting; Cognitive Skills; Questions [asking and/or responding]; Vocabulary Review)

Suggestion

Remember to use a pleasant conversational tone when speaking with the child.

MY OUCH STORY

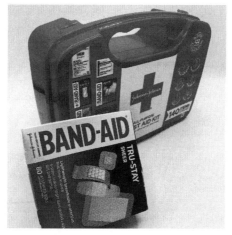

Figure 3.19.   My Ouch Story.

√	COMMUNICATION SKILL	√	COMMUNICATION SKILL
	Auxiliary Verbs		Pragmatics
	Cognitive Skills		Present Progressive Tense
√	Commentary, Questioning, Requesting		Present Tense Verbs
√	Concept Development		Requesting Assistance
	Future Tense (will)	√	Questions (asking and/or responding)
	Giving and Following Verbal Directives		Sequencing Skills
√	Modals	√	Vocabulary Development
	Negation	√	Vocabulary Review
√	Past Tense Verbs		

Time Needed for Activity: Approximately 15 to 30 minutes
Suggested Difficulty Level: #1
Suggested Concepts and Vocabulary:

- bandage
- hurt
- scrape
- injury

Materials:

- a box of Band-Aids or any other adhesive bandage

Procedure:

1. Give each participant a bandage to actually put on.
2. Tell the children that they can place the bandage wherever they choose. It is up to them. Some children may need assistance putting the bandage on.
3. Each participant will have a turn to tell how they got hurt.

Small Talk Suggestions:
Pre-Activity

- Give out the bandages, and ask/say:

    ○ "Who knows what I am giving out?" (Questions [asking and/or responding]; Vocabulary Development)
    ○ "That's right. This is a Band-Aid!" (Commentary, Questioning, Requesting; Vocabulary Development)
    ○ "What is a Band-Aid for?" (Questions [asking and/or responding]; Vocabulary Development)
    ○ "When did you need a Band-Aid?" (Questions [asking and/or responding])

During the Activity

- Once all of the children have their bandage affixed, encourage them to tell a story about when they needed a Band-Aid. Let them know that it is okay to make up a story, to make up a pretend story. Tell them that it is okay for them to use their imaginations.

    ○ "Would you please tell me how you got hurt?" (Modals; Questions [asking and/or responding])
    ○ "How did you get injured?" (Past Tense Verbs; Questions [asking and/or responding])
    ○ "I ran down the street and fell down!" (Commentary, Questioning, Requesting)
    ○ "I scraped my elbow." (Past Tense Verbs)
    ○ "My elbow felt sore." (Commentary, Questioning, Requesting)
    ○ "What happened to you, _____?" (Questions [asking and/or responding]; Past Tense Verbs)
    ○ "Wow! That story made me feel sad." (Concept Development)
    ○ "Do you feel better now?" (Questions [asking and/or responding])

Post-Activity

- Wrap up the activity with a discussion about safety.
  - "How can you keep from getting hurt again?" (Questions [asking and/or responding])
  - "What will you do if you fall and scrape your body?" (Questions [asking and/or responding]; Vocabulary Review)
  - "Should you tell someone if you get hurt?" (Modals; Questions [asking and/or responding])

Suggestion

Expand this activity to any adults in the classroom, such as the teacher, student intern, teacher's assistant, parent volunteer, etc. Let them get things started by telling the class about a time they ended up with an "ouchy."

I AM SO THANKFUL

√	COMMUNICATION SKILL	√	COMMUNICATION SKILL
√	Auxiliary Verbs		Pragmatics
	Cognitive Skills	√	Present Progressive Tense
	Commentary, Questioning, Requesting	√	Present Tense Verbs
√	Concept Development		Requesting Assistance
	Future Tense (will)	√	Questions (asking and/or responding)
√	Giving and Following Verbal Directives		Sequencing Skills
	Modals	√	Vocabulary Development
	Negation	√	Vocabulary Review
√	Past Tense Verbs		

Time Needed for Activity: Approximately 15 to 30 minutes
Difficulty Level: #1
Suggested Concepts and Vocabulary:

- thank you
- thankful

Materials:

- construction paper
- boxes of crayons

Procedure:

1. Tell the children about something that the teacher is thankful for, and explain why he/she is thankful.
2. Encourage the children to do some thinking about what they are thankful for.
3. Give each of the participants a box of crayons and a sheet of construction paper.
4. Instruct the children to draw a picture of something that they are thankful for.

Small Talk Suggestions:
Pre-Activity

- Stimulate a conversation about being thankful.

    ○ "What do you say when someone does something nice for you?" (Questions [asking and/or responding])

- ◦ "Do you say 'Thank you' to people who give you something nice?" (Auxiliary Verbs; Questions [asking and/or responding])
- ◦ "Ms. Smith says 'Thank you' when you hold the door open for her." (Present Tense Verbs)
- ◦ "I said, 'Thank you' to the doctor who gave me medicine to make me feel better." (Past Tense Verbs)
- ◦ "I feel thankful when my car works." (Present Tense Verbs)

During the Activity

- • Open the discussion to the children.
  - ◦ "When do you feel thankful?" (Questions [asking and/or responding]; Vocabulary Development)
  - ◦ "Do you feel happy or sad when you are thankful?" (Concept Development; Auxiliary Verbs; Questions [asking and/or responding]; Vocabulary Development)
  - ◦ "Did anyone ever say 'Thank you' to you?" (Past Tense Verbs; Vocabulary Development)
  - ◦ "Was anyone ever thankful for something nice that you did?" (Past Tense Verbs; Questions [asking and/or responding])
- • Have the children draw a picture of something that they are thankful for.
  - ◦ "Ask _____ to give you construction paper and crayons to draw a picture of what you are thankful for." (Giving and Following Verbal Directives; Questions [asking and/or responding])
  - ◦ "_____ is drawing a house." (Present Progressive Tense)
  - ◦ "_____ is drawing food." (Present Progressive Tense)

Post-Activity

- • Discussion/Circle Time
  - ◦ "Let's look at some of the pictures you drew about being thankful." (Past Tense Verbs; Vocabulary Review)
  - ◦ "_____ drew a picture of a new house. He is thankful." (Past Tense Verbs; Vocabulary Review)
  - ◦ "_____ drew a picture of her mother's new car. She is thankful." (Past Tense Verbs; Vocabulary Review)
  - ◦ "_____ drew a picture of food. She is thankful for food to eat." (Past Tense Verbs; Vocabulary Review)
  - ◦ "I drew a picture of all of you. I am thankful for your bright smiles!" (Past Tense Verbs; Vocabulary Review)

Suggestion

Talk to the class about thank-you cards and the importance of showing gratitude to those who do nice things for us. Think of someone who has been very kind to the class, then send that person a special thank-you note, either handmade or purchased from a store.

FAMILY MATTERS

√	COMMUNICATION SKILL	√	COMMUNICATION SKILL
√	Auxiliary Verbs		Pragmatics
	Cognitive Skills	√	Present Progressive Tense
	Commentary, Questioning, Requesting		Present Tense Verbs
√	Concept Development		Requesting Assistance
√	Future Tense (will)	√	Questions (asking and/or responding)
√	Giving and Following Verbal Directives		Sequencing Skills
√	Modals	√	Vocabulary Development
	Negation	√	Vocabulary Review
√	Past Tense Verbs		

Time Needed for Activity: Approximately 15 to 30 minutes
Difficulty Level: #1
Suggested Concepts and Vocabulary:

- family
- siblings
- brother
- sister
- grandparents
- grandfather
- grandmother
- youngest
- oldest

Materials:

- photographs of the teacher's family
- construction paper
- boxes of crayons

Procedure:

1. The teacher should tell the children about his/her family (parent[s], siblings, etc.).
2. Show photographs of the teacher's family members, including photos of the teacher as a child, especially at the age of the children in the class.
3. Give the children an opportunity to tell the class about their own families, including pets.

4. Provide the listeners an opportunity to ask questions about the speaker's family.
5. Provide construction paper and boxes of crayons for the children to draw pictures of their family members.

Small Talk Suggestions:
Pre-Activity

- Gather the children together in a circle or semicircle in the Circle Time area or in the class library, so all participants are comfortable.

    ◦ "Let's talk about some very special people in our lives, our families!" (Giving and Following Verbal Directives)
    ◦ "I will start first. Okay?" (Future Tense [will])

During the Activity

- The teacher should show the children photos of his/her family.

    ◦ "Who do you think these people are?" (Vocabulary Development)
    ◦ "These are members of my family." (Vocabulary Development)

- Turn the attention to the children. Ask each child to tell the class about their own family.

    ◦ "Tell us about your mother/father, your parents." (Vocabulary Development)
    ◦ "Do you have any siblings, brothers and sisters?" (Questions [asking and/or responding]; Vocabulary Development; Auxiliary Verbs)
    ◦ "Are any of your brothers and sisters older than you?" (Questions [asking and/or responding]; Concept Development; Vocabulary Development)
    ◦ "Are any of your brothers and sisters younger than you?" (Questions [asking and/or responding]; Concept Development; Vocabulary Development)
    ◦ "Who is the oldest?" (Questions [asking and/or responding]; Concept Development; Vocabulary Development)
    ◦ "Who is the youngest?" (Questions [asking and/or responding]; Concept Development; Vocabulary Development)
    ◦ "Do you have any pets?" (Questions [asking and/or responding]; Auxiliary Verbs)

- Encourage the children to draw a picture of their family.

    ◦ "Let's draw pictures of our families. Tell me what we will need." (Future Tense[will]; Vocabulary Development)
    ◦ "_____ should draw a picture of his/her cat in the family picture." (Modals)
    ◦ "_____ is coloring his brother's shirt green." (Present Progressive Tense)

Post-Activity

- Discuss the family pictures as the teacher is putting them up in the classroom display area.

    ○ "_____ has a big family." (Vocabulary Review)
    ○ "_____ has two siblings." (Vocabulary Review)
    ○ "_____ colored a picture of his grandparents." (Past Tense Verbs; Vocabulary Review)
    ○ "_____ pasted glitter on her mother's dress." (Past Tense Verbs)
    ○ "_____ made his pet dog big." (Past Tense Verbs; Concept Development; Vocabulary Review)
    ○ "_____ made her cat small." (Past Tense Verbs; Concept Development; Vocabulary Review)

Suggestion

Try not to anticipate the child's needs. Set up situations that require the child to speak, whether commenting or asking for something she/he needs or wants. Even if the child has limited language skills, the aim is to encourage her/him to use those skills to communicate with others in the environment.

FIND A HOUSE

√	COMMUNICATION SKILL	√	COMMUNICATION SKILL
	Auxiliary Verbs		Pragmatics
√	Cognitive Skills	√	Present Progressive Tense
	Commentary, Questioning, Requesting		Present Tense Verbs
√	Concept Development		Requesting Assistance
√	Future Tense (will)	√	Questions (asking and/or responding)
√	Giving and Following Verbal Directives		Sequencing Skills
	Modals	√	Vocabulary Development
	Negation	√	Vocabulary Review
	Past Tense Verbs		

Time Needed for Activity: Approximately 20 to 30 minutes
Difficulty Level: #1
Suggested Concepts and Vocabulary:

- tall
- short

Materials:

- as many individual photographs as possible of beautiful tall and short houses glued onto sheets of construction paper (enough photos for each participant, including any adults)

Procedure:

1. Display all of the house photos on a table or easel for the children to easily view.
2. Point out and talk about each of the tall houses.
3. Point out and talk about each of the short houses.
4. Tell the children to hide their eyes while the teacher hides one of the houses somewhere in the classroom.
5. When the children are instructed to open their eyes, they must search the room for the hidden house.
6. When a child finds the missing house, he/she must tell whether it is a tall house or a short house. She/He gets to keep the photograph.

Small Talk Suggestions:
Pre-Activity

- Draw the children's attention to the photos of the tall and short houses.

  - "Some of the houses are tall, and some are short." (Concept Development; Vocabulary Development)
  - "Would you like to live in a tall house or a short house?" (Questions [asking and/or responding]; Vocabulary Development; Concept Development)
  - "Which houses are tall?" (Questions [asking and/or responding]; Concept Development; Vocabulary Development)
  - "Which houses are short?" (Questions [asking and/or responding]; Concept Development; Vocabulary Development)

During the Activity

- Tell the children how to play the game.

  - "Let's play a game." (Giving and Following Verbal Directives)
  - "When you close your eyes, I will hide one of the houses. When I tell you to open your eyes, you get to look around the room for the hidden house. Okay?" (Future Tense [will]; Giving and Following Verbal Directives)
  - "Whoever finds the house can keep the picture." (Giving and Following Verbal Directives)
  - "Now, close your eyes!" (Giving and Following Verbal Directives; Concept Development)
  - "Now, open your eyes!" (Giving and Following Verbal Directives; Concept Development)
  - "_____ and _____ are looking for a new house." (Present Progressive Tense)
  - "I think some of you are getting closer and closer to a house." (Present Progressive Tense)

- Continue this procedure until each child has at least one house.

Post-Activity

- Gather all of the children together.

  - "Did we have fun?" (Questions [asking and/or responding])
  - "Did all of you get a house?" (Questions [asking and/or responding])
  - "How many houses did you find, _____?" (Questions [asking and/or responding]; Concept Development; Cognitive Skills)

- ○ "_____, what color is your house?" (Questions [asking and/or responding]; Concept Development)
- ○ "Who found a tall house?" (Questions [asking and/or responding]; Concept Development; Vocabulary Review)
- ○ "Who found a short house?" (Questions [asking and/or responding]; Concept Development; Vocabulary Review)
- ○ "Who has a tall house and a short house?" (Questions [asking and/or responding]; Concept Development; Vocabulary Review)

Suggestion

Expand upon the child's oral communication attempts by responding with an "expansion." For example:

- Child (pointing at a cat): Cat!
- Adult: Yes! That is a cat.

HUCKLE BUCKLE BEANSTALK

√	COMMUNICATION SKILL	√	COMMUNICATION SKILL
√	Auxiliary Verbs		Pragmatics
	Cognitive Skills	√	Present Progressive Tense
	Commentary, Questioning, Requesting		Present Tense Verbs
√	Concept Development		Requesting Assistance
√	Future Tense (will)	√	Questions (asking and/or responding)
√	Giving and Following Verbal Directives		Sequencing Skills
√	Modals		Vocabulary Development
	Negation		Vocabulary Review
√	Past Tense Verbs		

Time Needed for Activity: Approximately 20 to 30 minutes
Difficulty Level: #1
Suggested Concepts and Vocabulary:

- word(s) for the item(s) used to hide during the game

Materials:

- Any small object(s), such as a beanbag or a chalkboard eraser

Procedure:

1. Tell the children to either sit at their desks or on the floor in a circle.
2. Show the children the selected object for the game.
3. Once all of the children have seen the object, have them hide their eyes by just closing them or by putting their heads down.
4. Quietly walk around the room and hide the object. After the object is hidden, take a few more seconds to continue walking around, so the children will have no clue as to where the object is hidden.
5. When ready, tell the children, "Find it." The children must quietly search the room for the hidden object.
6. The child who finds the object can do one of two things:

   a. Grab the object, and yell, "Huckle Buckle Beanstalk," or
   b. Return to his/her seat and declare, "Huckle Buckle Beanstalk!" At this point, the hider of the object gives the child permission to retrieve the object.

7. The winner of the round gets to be the hider of the object in the next round of the game.

Small Talk Suggestions:
Pre-Activity

- Tell the children how Huckle Buckle Beanstalk is played.

    ◦ "What object should we hide?" (Questions [asking and/or responding])
    ◦ "What will you do when I say 'Close your eyes!'?" (Questions [asking and/or responding]; Future Tense [will])
    ◦ "What will you do when I say 'Open your eyes!'?" (Questions [asking and/or responding]; Future Tense [will])
    ◦ "If you are the one who sees the object, what will you do?" (Questions [asking and/or responding]; Future Tense [will])

During the Activity

- Engage the children in the activity.

    ◦ "Close your eyes!" (Giving and Following Verbal Directives; Concept Development)
    ◦ "Open your eyes!" (Giving and Following Verbal Directives; Concept Development)
    ◦ "Quietly look for the _____." (Giving and Following Verbal Directives)
    ◦ "_____ is rushing back to his/her seat!" (Present Progressive Tense)
    ◦ "I think _____ found the _____!" (Past Tense Verbs)

- Once a child finds the object, that individual gets to lead the next round and use the game's phrases.

Post-Activity

- "Did you enjoy our game today?" (Questions [asking and/or responding]; Auxiliary Verbs)
- "Can we play this game again one day?" (Questions [asking and/or responding]; Modals)

Suggestion

As appropriate circumstances arise, discuss similarities and differences as they occur, such as colors, shapes, textures, etc.

IS THAT A CIRCLE?

√	COMMUNICATION SKILL	√	COMMUNICATION SKILL
√	Auxiliary Verbs		Pragmatics
√	Cognitive Skills	√	Present Progressive Tense
	Commentary, Questioning, Requesting		Present Tense Verbs
√	Concept Development		Requesting Assistance
√	Future Tense (will)	√	Questions (asking and/or responding)
√	Giving and Following Verbal Directives		Sequencing Skills
√	Modals	√	Vocabulary Development
√	Negation	√	Vocabulary Review
√	Past Tense Verbs		

Time Needed for Activity: Approximately 20 to 30 minutes
Difficulty Level: #1
Suggested Concepts and Vocabulary:

- shapes
- circle
- square
- triangle
- rectangle

Materials:

- a bag or a large box
- small items of distinct shapes, including rectangles, triangles, squares, circles

Procedure:

1. Gather the children together in a close circle.
2. Tell the children that there are lots of objects in the big bag/box, and the items are all different shapes.
3. The teacher or another participating adult should reach into the bag/box and take out an item.
4. The teacher should ask, "What shape is that?"
5. The other adult should correctly identify the item's shape.
6. The participating adult should reach into the bag/box and intentionally pull out an item of a different shape.
7. The teacher again asks, "What shape is that?"

8. This procedure should continue until an adult has identified each of the four shapes included in this activity.

9. Next, each child should have a few turns taking an item from the bag and identifying its shape.

Small Talk Suggestions:
Pre-Activity

- Shake the bag/box for the children, to stimulate their interest.

  ◦ "Do you know what I have in this bag/box?" (Auxiliary Verbs; Questions [asking and/or responding])
  ◦ "I have different shapes in here." (Concept Development; Vocabulary Development)
  ◦ "I have circles and squares and triangles and rectangles in this bag/box." (Concept Development)
  ◦ "Let's guess all of the shapes in the bag/box!" (Concept Development; Giving and Following Verbal Directives)
  ◦ "You will put your hand in the bag/box, then take an object out of the bag/box." (Future Tense [will]; Giving and Following Verbal Directives)
  ◦ "Next, guess what shape it is." (Concept Development; Cognitive Skills)

During the Activity

- Engage the children in the guessing game.

  ◦ "_____ is putting his/her hand in the bag/box." (Present Progressive Tense)
  ◦ "_____ is taking something out of the bag/box." (Present Progressive Tense)
  ◦ "What shape is it?" (Questions [asking and/or responding]; Concept Development)
  ◦ "Can you guess what this shape is?" (Modals; Questions [asking and/or responding]; Vocabulary Development)
  ◦ "Wow! That's right. It's a (shape)!" (Concept Development; Vocabulary Development)
  ◦ "Oh, no! That's not a (error shape). That's a (target shape)." (Negation; Concept Development; Vocabulary Development)
  ◦ "Who is next?" (Questions [asking and/or responding])

Post-Activity

- Wrap up the activity with a discussion about the activity.
  - "What did we talk about today?" (Questions [and and/or responding]; Vocabulary Review)
  - "We talked about shapes." (Past Tense Verbs)
  - "Who remembers the shapes that we found in the bag/box?" (Questions [asking and/or responding]; Vocabulary Review)
  - "Yes, we found circles, squares, triangles, and rectangles." (Vocabulary Review)
  - "Let's look around the room for things shaped like a (circle/square/triangle/rectangle)." (Vocabulary Review; Giving and Following Verbal Directives)

Suggestion

Do the same activity at a later date, but use another shape as the target shape, such as the square, the rectangle, etc.

PASS THE PARCEL

Figure 3.20.   Pass the Parcel.

√	COMMUNICATION SKILL	√	COMMUNICATION SKILL
	Auxiliary Verbs		Pragmatics
	Cognitive Skills	√	Present Progressive Tense
	Commentary, Questioning, Requesting	√	Present Tense Verbs
√	Concept Development		Requesting Assistance
	Future Tense (will)	√	Questions (asking and/or responding)
√	Giving and Following Verbal Directives		Sequencing Skills
√	Modals	√	Vocabulary Development
	Negation	√	Vocabulary Review
√	Past Tense Verbs		

Time Needed for Activity: Approximately 20 to 30 minutes
Difficulty Level: #1
Suggested Concepts and Vocabulary:

- music
- listen
- on
- stop
- pass
- parcel
- words for the trinkets/treats in the parcel

Materials:

- shoe box with lid
- enough trinkets/small toys that will fit into the box for each player
- five or more rolls of various patterns and colors of wrapping paper
- tape
- music on a device that can be easily turned on and off

Procedure:

1. Place all of the trinkets/toys into the shoe box.
2. Place the lid on the box.
3. Select a wrapping paper, and wrap the box.
4. Select a different wrapping paper, then wrap the box again. Keep wrapping the same box with different wrapping for the number of rounds the game is expected to run. Be certain to use wrapping papers of very different patterns and colors to make it easy for the players to tell them apart.
5. Instruct the children to either sit on the floor or on chairs in a circle.
6. Turn on the music.
7. Instruct the children to pass the box from one child to the next as the music is playing. Tell them to listen carefully for the music.
8. Tell the children that when they hear the music stop, whoever has the box in his/her hands gets to remove one layer of wrapping paper—only one layer. This is why it is important for the layers to be clearly wrapped in paper of varying patterns and colors.
9. Continue the game until the music stops, and a child opens the last layer of wrapping paper. That child gets to open the box (the parcel) and be the first to choose a gift inside.
10. Next, the other children get their chance to select a trinket.

Small Talk Suggestions:
Pre-Activity

- Explain the activity to the children. Have the wrapped box at hand to show them, and shake the box, so the children hear the prizes within.
  - "When I turn the music on, keep passing the parcel to your left/right." (Giving and Following Verbal Directives; Concept Development; Vocabulary Development)
  - "When the music stops, whoever is holding the box gets to take one layer of paper off." (Giving and Following Verbal Directives; Vocabulary Development)

During the Activity

- Start the music.
  - "Listen to the music, and pass the parcel to the left/right." (Giving and Following Verbal Directives; Concept Development; Vocabulary Development)
  - "_____ is passing the parcel to his/her left/right." (Present Progressive Tense; Concept Development; Vocabulary Development)
  - "_____ is listening to the music." (Present Progressive Tense)

- Stop the music.
  - "I stopped the music, and who has the box?" (Past Tense Verbs; Vocabulary Development; Questions [asking and/or responding])
  - "Wow! _____ is holding the parcel! You get to take some paper off the box!" (Present Progressive Tense; Giving and Following Verbal Directives)
  - "_____ unwraps the paper." (Present Tense Verbs; Vocabulary Development)

Note: Depending upon the child's fine motor skill level, the teacher may need to assist the child in removing only one layer of wrapping paper.

- Select a direction for the box to be passed, and continue the music.
  - "Now, let's pass the box to the left/right." (Concept Development; Giving and Following Verbal Directives; Vocabulary Development)

- Continue this procedure until a child finally unwraps the final layer of wrapping paper.
  - "_____ is opening the parcel for the class." (Present Progressive Tense)
  - "What is inside?" (Questions [asking and/or responding])
  - "_____ is selecting a trinket." (Present Progressive Tense)

Post-Activity

- During Discussion/Circle Time:
  - "What game did we play today?" (Questions [asking and/or responding])
  - "What did we pass from one person to the next?" (Vocabulary Review; Questions [asking and/or responding])
  - "We passed the parcel from one person to the next." (Past Tense Verbs)
  - "_____ passed the box to the left/right." (Past Tense Verbs; Concept Development)
  - "Can we play this game again one day?" (Modals; Questions [asking and/or responding])

Suggestion

Incorporate a discussion of daily experiences in the class's Circle Time at the end of the school day. This could be an ideal time to talk about things that happened, good or not so good. Encourage the children to share their opinions as others listen without judgment. Encourage them to help one another solve problems as a team.

SKIPPYROO KANGAROO

√	COMMUNICATION SKILL	√	COMMUNICATION SKILL
	Auxiliary Verbs		Pragmatics
	Cognitive Skills	√	Present Progressive Tense
	Commentary, Questioning, Requesting		Present Tense Verbs
√	Concept Development		Requesting Assistance
√	Future Tense (will)	√	Questions (asking and/or responding)
√	Giving and Following Verbal Directives		Sequencing Skills
√	Modals	√	Vocabulary Development
√	Negation	√	Vocabulary Review
√	Past Tense Verbs		

Time Needed for Activity: Approximately 20 to 30 minutes
Difficulty Level: #1
Suggested Concepts and Vocabulary:

- kangaroo

Materials: None

Procedure:

1. Have the children sit in a circle, either on the floor or in chairs.
2. Select one child to sit or stand in the middle of the circle. This child is "Skippyroo, the Kangaroo."
3. Skippyroo must hide her/his eyes.
4. Now, as Skippyroo hides her/his eyes, the other children chant, "Skippyroo, kangaroo, dozing in the midday sun, comes a hunter, run, run, run!"
5. The teacher selects one of the children to silently go over to Skippyroo (eyes still hidden), tap him/her on the shoulder, and say, "Guess who caught you just for fun."
6. Skippyroo must guess the name of the child who tapped him/her just by voice recognition.
7. If Skippyroo guesses correctly, he/she joins the children in the circle while the child whose name was guessed has a chance to be the next Skippyroo.
8. If Skippyroo guesses incorrectly, he/she may have one more guess. If Skippyroo still cannot guess the correct name of the child, he/she may open his/her eyes to see who the child is. The child standing behind Skippyroo gets to be the new Skippyroo Kangaroo.
9. Let this game continue until each child has had an opportunity to be Skippyroo.

Small Talk Suggestions:
Pre-Activity

- Explain the game to the children.

  ○ "For this game, each Skippyroo Kangaroo has to listen carefully to recognize voices." (Giving and Following Verbal Directives)

  ○ "Let's sit in a circle, and _____ will be our first Skippyroo." (Future Tense [will]; Giving and Following Verbal Directives)

- Show the children various photographs of kangaroos.

  ○ "Do you know what animal this is?" (Questions [asking and/or responding])

  ○ "This is called a kangaroo." (Vocabulary Development)

  ○ "The baby kangaroo is called a joey." (Vocabulary Development)

  ○ "Look at this picture. The joey is in the mother kangaroo's pouch!" (Vocabulary Development)

During the Activity

- Start the game.

  ○ "Say this with me, 'Skippyroo, kangaroo, dozing in the midday sun, comes a hunter, run, run, run!'" (Giving and Following Verbal Directives)

  ○ "Okay, Skippyroo. Close your eyes!" (Giving and Following Verbal Directives; Concept Development)

- Select a child to silently stand behind Skippyroo.

  ○ "Now, tap Skippyroo on the shoulder, and say, 'Guess who caught you just for fun.'" (Giving and Following Verbal Directives)

  ○ "Okay, Skippyroo! Guess who said that." (Past Tense Verbs; Giving and Following Verbal Directives)

  ○ "_____ is trying to guess whose voice he/she heard." (Present Progressive Tense; Past Tense Verbs)

- If Skippyroo guesses incorrectly:

  ○ "No! Guess again!" (Negation)

Post-Activity

- After the game is concluded, use a few minutes to stay in a circle, and talk about the game.

  ○ "Would you like to play Skippyroo Kangaroo again one day?" (Modals; Questions [asking and/or responding])

  ○ "_____ made good guesses!" (Past Tense Verbs)

- • Present the photos of the kangaroos again. Have other pictures, too, that were not previously shown to the children. Talk about the pictures, and instruct the children to point to the items that are mentioned. (Vocabulary Review)

Suggestion

Discuss cause-and-effect situations that the children can relate well to, such as, "What could happen if you play with matches?"

NATURE WALK

√	COMMUNICATION SKILL	√	COMMUNICATION SKILL
	Auxiliary Verbs		Pragmatics
	Cognitive Skills	√	Present Progressive Tense
	Commentary, Questioning, Requesting	√	Present Tense Verbs
√	Concept Development		Requesting Assistance
√	Future Tense (will)	√	Questions (asking and/or responding)
	Giving and Following Verbal Directives		Sequencing Skills
√	Modals	√	Vocabulary Development
√	Negation	√	Vocabulary Review
√	Past Tense Verbs		

Time Needed for the Activity: Approximately 2 hours
Difficulty Level: #1
Suggested Concepts and Vocabulary:

- leaves
- trees
- insect
- squirrel
- rock
- pebble
- words for any encountered items of nature

Materials:

- digital camera

Procedure:

1. Plan this field trip for a warm day, preferably during a spring or autumn afternoon. Ideally, this walking trip should take place in a nearby park, but a nature walk through the school's neighborhood would be fine.
2. Tell the children that they should be on the lookout for things in nature.
3. Tell the children what it means to observe their surroundings.
4. Explain to the children that they must look for birds, plants, rocks, squirrels, chipmunks, and other interesting things in nature.
5. Instruct the children to alert the teacher to interesting things to take pictures of for the classroom display.

Small Talk Suggestions:
Pre-Activity

- Prepare the children for the walk in the park.

  ○ "Can you think of a place where we can go to see lots of trees, birds, plants, and rocks?" (Questions [asking and/or responding]; Vocabulary Development)
  ○ "We are going to the park." (Present Progressive Tense)
  ○ "What do you think we will see in the park?" (Questions [asking and/or responding]; Vocabulary Development)
  ○ "We will take pictures of interesting things in the park." (Future Tense [will])

During the Activity

- Talk about interesting items that the children observe in the park.

  ○ "_____ is observing the pretty robins as they fly." (Present Progressive Tense; Vocabulary Development)
  ○ "Will we find some acorns to take back to school?" (Future Tense [will]; Questions [asking and/or responding])
  ○ "_____ is taking pictures of big trees and small trees." (Present Progressive Tense)
  ○ "Do you see the lake, _____? I wonder if we can see any fish in the lake." (Modals; Questions [asking and/or responding])
  ○ "What colors do you see in the flowers?" (Concept Development; Questions [asking and/or responding])
  ○ "A beautiful butterfly landed on the flower." (Concept Development; Past Tense Verbs)
  ○ "The bumblebee is buzzing around the flowers." (Present Progressive Tense)
  ○ "_____ loves insects!" (Present Tense Verbs)
  ○ "The teacher does not like insects. He/She is afraid of insects." (Negation)

- Continue narrating the observations of the children as they occur, and do not forget to take plenty of photographs of each thing the children take special note of.

Post-Activity

- A soon as possible, print out a number of significant photographs connected to the nature walk through the park. Use them to prompt conversation about the field trip.

  ○ "Where did we go to observe nature?" (Questions [asking and/or responding])
  ○ "_____, tell me what you saw in the park." (Past Tense Verbs; Vocabulary Review)

- ○ "We enjoyed watching the butterfly landing on the flowers." (Past Tense Verbs; Vocabulary Review)
- ○ "The bumblebee buzzed all around us." (Past Tense Verbs; Vocabulary Review)
- ○ "_____ saw a bug crawling on the ground." (Past Tense Verbs; Vocabulary Review)
- ○ "_____ brought back some big leaves and little leaves." (Past Tense Verbs; Vocabulary Review)
- ○ "_____ collected some bumpy rocks and small pebbles." (Past Tense Verbs; Vocabulary Review)
- ○ "_____ wants to put up our nature walk photographs in our classroom library." (Present Tense Verbs)
- ○ "Who wants to display all of the things we brought back to school from the park?" (Questions [asking and/or responding])

Suggestion

Try asking questions that require more than a yes or no response from the child. Instead, ask the child, "What is happening in the picture?" or "Tell me about it."

INTERMEDIATE ACTIVITIES

These activities (Difficulty Level #2) are considered best for young learners with some experience with fine motor control/coordination and require minimal hand-over-hand assistance.

I CAN'T BELIEVE IT'S BUTTER!

Figure 4.1.   I Can't Believe It's Butter!

√	COMMUNICATION SKILL	√	COMMUNICATION SKILL
	Auxiliary Verbs	√	Pragmatics
√	Cognitive Skills	√	Present Progressive Tense
	Commentary, Questioning, Requesting	√	Present Tense Verbs
√	Concept Development	√	Requesting Assistance
√	Future Tense (will)	√	Questions (asking and/or responding)
√	Giving and Following Verbal Directives		Sequencing Skills
	Modals	√	Vocabulary Development
√	Negation	√	Vocabulary Review
√	Past Tense Verbs		

Time Needed for Activity: Approximately 45 minutes to 1 hour
Difficulty Level: #2
Suggested Concepts and Vocabulary:

- cream
- jar
- lid
- crackers
- butter
- knife

- salt
- shake
- spread
- eat
- in/on
- open/close

Materials:

- one glass or plastic jar (approximately 2 lbs., 8 oz.), such as a small mayonnaise or peanut butter jar with a lid, per child (make sure the container is one that the children can see through during the butter-making process)
- a quart container of heavy cream/whipping cream (or more depending upon how many children are participating)
- a box of crackers or bread (crunchy, flavorful crackers are the BEST!)
- butter knives, one for each child
- napkins
- salt (optional)

Procedure:

1. Help the children pour the heavy cream into the jar so it is about half full, and add a dash of salt to taste, if desired. Secure the lid tightly.
2. Let the children shake their jars vigorously. Take turns with them, as this process may take quite a few minutes. Continual, vigorous shaking should yield butter in about 10 to 11 minutes. Continue shaking the jars until you see the heavy cream beginning to solidify into a chunk of butter.
3. When the butter is ready, open the jars just enough to pour off any remaining liquid (aka buttermilk). The buttermilk can be saved for use in baking sweet treats.
4. Spread some butter on the crackers or bread for a snack. Enjoy!

Activity Variation: As an alternative to providing individual jars to each child, it may be advantageous to have one jar with heavy cream for the teacher to shake. She/He can get the process going by shaking the heavy cream until it starts to change to butter, then let each child take a turn shaking the jar. When the jar makes its rounds and comes back to the teacher, she/he can finish the process by shaking the jar to complete the butter. Since the butter-making process can take quite a while, there is the possibility of losing students' attention if they do their own jar shaking. The heavy cream should convert to butter with rigorous shaking in 10 to 11 minutes.

Small Talk Suggestions:
Pre-Activity

- Place all of the materials for the activity on a table in plain view of the children. Ask, "What do you think we are going to make?" (Questions [asking and/or responding]; Cognitive Skills)
- "Who can tell me what I brought in today?" (Questions [asking and/or responding]; Vocabulary Development)

During the Activity

- Note: During the activity, use self-talk to narrate your actions. For example:
  - "We will open the jars." (Concept Development; Future Tense [will])
  - "I'm pouring the heavy cream into the jar." (Present Progressive Tense)
  - "Pour the cream into the jar. (Giving and Following Verbal Directives)
  - "Remember to close the lid." (Concept Development; Giving and Following Verbal Directives)
  - "I'm spreading the butter on a cracker." (Present Progressive Tense)
  - "Who likes butter?" (Questions [asking and/or responding]; Present Tense Verbs)
  - "Shake, shake, shake your jar!" (Giving and Following Verbal Directives)
  - "What will happen to the cream?" (Questions [asking and/or responding]; Cognitive Skills)
  - "What can we spread butter on?" (Questions [asking and/or responding])
  - "Spread some butter on your crackers." (Giving and Following Verbal Directives)

- Give the children their jars and lids, but "forget" to pour the heavy cream into the jars and tell them to start shaking the cream. Wait to see who calls for help. (Requesting Assistance)

Post-Activity

- Upon completion of the activity, try stimulating a discussion by using any one or more of the following questions and/or comments:
  - "Where do you think heavy cream comes from?" (Cognitive Skills; Questions [asking and/or responding])
  - "What does heavy cream look like?" (Concept Development; Questions [asking and/or responding])
  - "What color is our butter?" (Concept Development; Questions [asking and/or responding])

- ○ "What do you think will happen if we use plain milk to make our butter instead of heavy cream/whipping cream?" (Questions [asking and/or responding]; Cognitive Skills)
- ○ "What did you like about making butter?" (Questions [asking and/or responding]; Past Tense Verbs)
- ○ "What didn't you like about making butter?" (Questions [asking and/or responding]; Past Tense Verbs)
- ○ "_____ does not like butter." (Negation)
- ○ "What ingredients did we need to make butter?" (Questions [asking and/or responding]; Past Tense Verbs; Vocabulary Review)
- ○ "What other foods can we spread our butter on?" (Questions [asking and/or responding]; Vocabulary Development)
- ○ "What do you think would happen to the butter if we put too much salt in the butter?" (Questions [asking and/or responding]; Cognitive Skills)
- ○ "How are heavy cream and milk the same? How are they different?" (Questions [asking and/or responding]; Concept Development)
- ○ "What other things can we spread on crackers/bread?" (Questions [asking and/or responding]; Vocabulary Development)
- ○ "_____ poured the cream into the jar." (Past Tense Verbs)

- Invite another teacher or adult to the classroom, and ask the children to tell the invited guest(s) what they did in class.

  - ○ "Tell Mr./Ms. _____ what we did to make butter." (Pragmatics)

Suggestions

- Talk about other foods that butter tastes good on or in. Save some of the butter from the butter-making activity for use during lunchtime. It might be tasty on rolls or hot vegetables.
- Do a taste test. Spread some store-bought butter on a cracker and some of the homemade butter on another cracker. Let the children taste each one to compare the two. Ask them which one they liked best and why.

HEY THERE, CUPCAKE!

Figure 4.2.   Hey There, Cupcake!

√	COMMUNICATION SKILL	√	COMMUNICATION SKILL
√	Auxiliary Verbs	√	Pragmatics
√	Cognitive Skills	√	Present Progressive Tense
	Commentary, Questioning, Requesting	√	Present Tense Verbs
√	Concept Development		Requesting Assistance
	Future Tense (will)	√	Questions (asking and/or responding)
√	Giving and Following Verbal Directives	√	Sequencing Skills
√	Modals	√	Vocabulary Development
√	Negation	√	Vocabulary Review
	Past Tense Verbs		

Time Needed for Activity: Approximately 30 to 40 minutes
Difficulty Level: #2
Suggested Concepts and Vocabulary:

- cupcake
- frosting
- plates
- butter knife
- tablespoon
- container
- sprinkles
- spread
- stir
- sprinkle

Materials:

- 1 to 2 packs of store-bought cupcakes, any flavor, but without icing (enough for each participant)
- containers of prepared frosting, at room temperature (different flavors)
- chocolate or multicolor sprinkles
- plate for each child
- a butter knife or tablespoon

Procedure:

1. Open the packs of cupcakes, and place one on each plate.
2. Open the container of frosting, and allow each child a moment to stir just a bit. The more stirring at room temperature, the easier the frosting will spread on the cupcakes.
3. Using either the butter knife or a tablespoon, place a dollop of frosting on top of each cupcake; spread the frosting on the cupcakes.
4. Garnish the cupcake frosting with chocolate or multicolor sprinkles.
5. Let's eat!!!!

Activity Variation: Depending upon the temperature of the frosting, it may be so stiff that it causes large bits of the cupcake to tear away. A good idea might be to have a pack of cookies ready to replace the cupcakes. In fact, it is okay to plan the activity with cookies instead of cupcakes!

Small Talk Suggestions:
Pre-Activity

- One at a time, place each activity item on the table for the children to see, and ask:

  - "What do you think we are going to make?" (Cognitive Skills; Vocabulary Development)
  - "Who knows what this is?" (Vocabulary Development)
  - "Do you like cupcakes?" (Auxiliary Verbs; Vocabulary Development)

During the Activity

- Show the children how to stir the frosting.

  - "Would you like to stir?" (Modals)
  - "Who is stirring the frosting?" (Present Progressive Tense)
  - "_____ does not like chocolate." (Negation)

- ○ "What frosting flavor do you like the most?" (Questions [asking and responding]; Vocabulary Development)
- ○ "_____ is spreading frosting on the cupcake." (Present Progressive Tense)
- ○ "_____ is spreading vanilla frosting on top of the cupcake." (Concept Development; Present Progressive Tense)
- ○ "_____ spreads vanilla frosting on the bottom of his/her cupcake!" (Present Tense Verbs)

- • While performing the activity, emphasize the colors of the frostings selected for the cupcakes. Ask the child to find an item in the room that matches the color of the frosting.

  - ○ "Who can find something in this room that is the same color as the chocolate frosting (vanilla, strawberry, etc.)?" (Questions [asking and/or responding]; Concept Development; Vocabulary Development)

- • During the activity, the teacher performs the entire activity (opening the frosting can, stirring the frosting, opening the pack of cupcakes, frosting a cupcake as the children observe), talking about each step during demonstration. Next, the children should perform the activity as the teacher provides simple verbal directives for each step. (Giving and Following Verbal Directives; Sequencing Skills; Vocabulary Development)

Post-Activity

- • One by one, hold up each activity item for frosting the cupcakes and ask/say:

  - ○ "What is this? What did we do with this?" (Questions [asking and/or responding]; Vocabulary Review)
  - ○ "Let's tell _____ what we made today." (Pragmatics; Vocabulary Review; Past Tense Verbs)
  - ○ "How are a cupcake and a birthday cake the same (different)?" (Questions [asking and/or responding]; Cognitive Skills; Vocabulary Review)
  - ○ "What two words do you hear in 'cupcake'?" (Questions [asking and responding]; Vocabulary Review)

Suggestion

Encourage parents to closely supervise the child's television viewing habits. TV does not have to be eliminated, though. Watch TV with the child, and discuss what is being viewed. Talk about the plot, what is happening, what will happen, characters, the difference between fact and fiction, etc.

LET'S MAKE PEANUT BUTTER

Allergy Alert: Be Certain That None of Your Children Has an Allery to Peanuts!

Figure 4.3.   Let's Make Peanut Butter.

√	COMMUNICATION SKILL	√	COMMUNICATION SKILL
	Auxiliary Verbs		Pragmatics
√	Cognitive Skills	√	Present Progressive Tense
√	Commentary, Questioning, Requesting		Present Tense Verbs
	Concept Development		Requesting Assistance
√	Future Tense (will)	√	Questions (asking and/or responding)
	Giving and Following Verbal Directives		Sequencing Skills
√	Modals	√	Vocabulary Development
	Negation	√	Vocabulary Review
√	Past Tense Verbs		

Time Needed for Activity: Approximately 40 minutes
Difficulty Level: #2
Suggested Concepts and Vocabulary:

- peanut butter
- peanuts
- peanut oil
- food processor or blender (preferably a blender with the ability to pulse)
- bowl
- spoon
- measuring cup

- measuring spoon
- mix
- measure

Materials:

- About 1½ cups of roasted peanuts, unsalted, shelled (use more depending upon the size of the class)
- 1 to 2 tablespoons of peanut oil
- bread, crackers, or slices of apple
- food processor (a kitchen blender is most reliable)
- bowl
- spoon
- lidded storage container
- measuring cups
- measuring spoons

Procedure:

1. Pour the peanuts into the bowl of the blender, and pour about 1 tablespoon of the peanut oil on top.
2. Pulse the blender to chop up the peanuts. Add more peanut oil as needed.
3. Pulse until the mixture is the consistency of peanut butter. If it appears too dry, add more oil. If the mixture if too moist, add a few more peanuts.
4. Spread the peanut butter on bread, crackers, or slices of apple. Store the rest in the lidded container.

Small Talk Suggestions:
Pre-Activity

- Set up all of the equipment and ingredients for the children to see. Highlight each item:

  - "What did I bring in today?" (Questions [asking and/or responding]; Vocabulary Development)
  - "Who can tell me what we are going to make today?" (Questions [asking and/or responding]; Cognitive Skills; Vocabulary Development)
  - "_____, can you eat peanuts?" (Questions [asking and/or responding]; Modals)

During the Activity

- As the teacher and the children measure the peanuts and pour them into the food processor, say/ask:

  - "_____ is measuring the peanuts we need." (Present Progressive Tense; Vocabulary Development)
  - "We need a measuring spoon." (Commentary, Questioning, Requesting)
  - "Who will pour the peanuts into the food processor?" (Questions [asking and/ or responding]; Future Tense [will])
  - "What will happen to the peanuts in the food processor?" (Questions [asking and/or responding]; Future Tense [will]; Cognitive Skills)
  - "Who will turn the food processor on?" (Questions [asking and/or responding])
  - "Who does not like peanut butter?" (Questions [asking and/or responding]; Negation)

- As various children help in the process of pouring/stirring, say/ask:

  - "_____, what are you doing?" (Questions [asking and/or responding]; Vocabulary Development)
  - "_____ is pouring/stirring." (Present Progressive Tense)

Post-Activity

- During Circle Time

  - "What did we make today?" (Questions [asking and/or responding]; Past Tense Verbs; Vocabulary Review)
  - "Did we spread the peanuts or peanut butter on our crackers/bread?" (Questions [asking and/or responding]; Past Tense Verbs; Vocabulary Review)
  - "Who poured the peanuts into the food processor?" (Questions [asking and/or responding]; Past Tense Verbs; Vocabulary Review)
  - "Who stirred the peanut butter?" (Questions [asking and/or responding]; Past Tense Verbs; Vocabulary Review)

Suggestion

Try making the peanut butter by starting with fresh peanuts still in the shell. Show the children how peanuts look in their natural state. Teach them how to remove the peanuts from their shells and drop them into the blender/food processor.

COLORED SALT

Figure 4.4. Colored Salt.

Figure 4.5. Colored Salt.

√	COMMUNICATION SKILL	√	COMMUNICATION SKILL
	Auxiliary Verbs		Pragmatics
√	Cognitive Skills	√	Present Progressive Tense
√	Commentary, Questioning, Requesting		Present Tense Verbs
√	Concept Development	√	Requesting Assistance
√	Future Tense (will)	√	Questions (asking and/or responding)
√	Giving and Following Verbal Directives		Sequencing Skills
	Modals	√	Vocabulary Development
	Negation	√	Vocabulary Review
√	Past Tense Verbs		

Time Needed for Activity: Approximately 30 minutes
Difficulty Level: #2
Suggested Concepts and Vocabulary:

- salt
- chalk
- bowl
- letters of the alphabet
- words for numerals

Materials:

- A container of coarse table salt
- medium or large bowl for each child

- a box of colored chalk (the thick type used for street games, such as hopscotch)
- one serving tray with a lip around the perimeter (Look into borrowing enough trays for each activity participant from the school lunchroom. The lip will help contain the salt when poured onto the tray.)

Procedure:

1. Place the bowl in the tray so any spills will be contained, making cleanup easier.
2. Pour the salt into the bowl.
3. Encourage the children to select a piece of colored chalk. Help them hold the chalk and press in gently while making scribbling movements (circular movements work best) against the bottom and sides of the bowl. Make sure the child maintains firm but gentle pressure. Keep at it for a while, and watch as the salt turns to the color of the chalk.

Small Talk Suggestions:
Pre-Activity

- Place all of the materials on the table, and ask the children to figure out what the activity will be. Talk about the selected items.
  - "What did I bring in today?" (Questions [asking and/or responding]; Vocabulary Development)
  - "Do you know what we will be doing today?" (Questions [asking and/or responding]; Cognitive Skills; Future Tense [will])

During the Activity

- Instruct different children to give out the materials for the activity.
  - "Ask _____ to give you a tray (bowl, chalk)." (Questions [asking and/or responding]; Vocabulary Development)
  - "_____, may I have a (activity item)?" (Requesting Assistance)
  - "_____ is pouring salt into his/her bowl." (Present Progressive Tense)
  - "What color chalk do you have, _____?" (Concept Development)
- Model the chalk activity for the children.
  - "Watch me, and do what I do. Can you push the chalk down, and swirl it around in the salt?" (Giving and Following Verbal Directives)
  - "Move the chalk around like you are scribbling with a crayon." (Giving and Following Verbal Directives)
  - "I have blue chalk. What color will my salt be?" (Questions [asking and/or responding]; Cognitive Skills; Concept Development)

- ○ "_____, what is your favorite color?" (Questions [asking and/or responding]; Commentary, Questioning, Requesting; Concept Development)

- Once everyone has made some colored chalk, help the children pour some of their chalk onto their individual trays, then place the bowl of leftover salt to the side, or push the leftover colored salt to the center of the worktable. Help the children to gently shake their trays from side to side to evenly distribute the colored salt.

  - ○ "Who is pouring the salt?" (Questions [asking and/or responding]; Present Progressive Tense)
  - ○ "Let's make designs. Press your finger into your salt, and push it all the way to the tray. Now, carefully make some scribbles." (Giving and Following Verbal Directives)
  - ○ "Let's make some shapes. Make a circle (square, triangle, rectangle, diamond)." (Concept Development; Giving and Following Verbal Directives)
  - ○ "Can you print your initial(s) in your colored salt?" (Questions [asking and/or responding]; Cognitive Skills)
  - ○ "Can you spell your first name in your colored salt?" (Questions [asking and/or responding]; Cognitive Skills)
  - ○ "Print a number in your colored salt." (Cognitive Skills)
  - ○ "Print how old you are." (Cognitive Skills)
  - ○ "Can you print your age in your colored salt?" (Questions [asking and/or responding]; Concept Development)

Post-Activity

- As the teacher wraps up the activity, ask or say:

  - ○ "I saw lots of pretty colors used for your colored salt. What was your favorite color, _____?" (Concept Development; Questions [asking and/or responding]; Vocabulary Review; Past Tense Verbs)
  - ○ "Tell me the shapes that you made." (Past Tense Verbs; Commentary, Questioning, Requesting; Vocabulary Development; Vocabulary Review)

Suggestion

As the child expresses interest in knowing the names of various objects in the environment, use an index card to print the name of the item, then tape the label to the object.

MAKE A TAMBOURINE

Figure 4.6.   Making a Tambourine, View A.   **Figure 4.7.   Making a Tambourine, View B.**

√	COMMUNICATION SKILL	√	COMMUNICATION SKILL
	Auxiliary Verbs		Pragmatics
√	Cognitive Skills	√	Present Progressive Tense
	Commentary, Questioning, Requesting	√	Present Tense Verbs
√	Concept Development		Requesting Assistance
√	Future Tense (will)	√	Questions (asking and/or responding)
√	Giving and Following Verbal Directives	√	Sequencing Skills
	Modals	√	Vocabulary Development
	Negation	√	Vocabulary Review
√	Past Tense Verbs		

Time Needed for Activity: Approximately 1 hour
Difficulty Level: #2
Suggested Concepts and Vocabulary:

- tambourine
- paper plates
- beans
- glue
- paint

Materials:

- a small handful of dried beans
- 2 firm/heavy paper plates per child
- Elmer's glue
- tempera paints
- Mod Podge

Procedure:

1. Place one of the paper plates on the table.
2. Pour some dried beans in the plate.
3. Put some glue around the edge of the plate, then turn the other paper plate over, and place it on top of the first paper plate. Press the edges together to make sure there are no gaps. Let the glue dry for a bit.
4. After the glue has dried, use the tempera paints to paint the tambourine. Add glitter and some colorful stickers to decorate the new musical instrument.
5. When the tambourine dries, think of some good songs to sing, and help the children use the tambourine to beat to the rhythm.

Small Talk Suggestions:
Pre-Activity

- Show the children a completed tambourine. Shake it to a beat. Sing a short song, and hit the tambourine to that beat.

  - "What do you think we are making today?" (Questions [asking and/or responding]; Cognitive Skills; Vocabulary Development)

- Read a list of supplies for the activity, and instruct the children to look around the room, and retrieve the items.

  - "We will need paper plates (glue, paints, dry beans, etc.)" (Future Tense [will]; Giving and Following Verbal Directives; Vocabulary Development)

During the Activity

- Engage the children in the activity.

  - "_____ is pouring dry beans into the bottom paper plate." (Present Progressive Tense)
  - "_____ puts glue on the rim of the bottom paper plate." (Present Tense Verbs)

- "I am gluing the top paper plate to the bottom paper plate. Watch me." (Present Progressive Tense; Giving and Following Verbal Directives)
- "Gently press the top paper plate against the bottom paper plate, so they will stick together." (Giving and Following Verbal Directives; Future Tense [will])
- "_____ is painting his/her tambourine red." (Present Progressive Tense; Concept Development)
- "_____, what color will you paint your tambourine?" (Questions [asking and/or responding]; Concept Development; Future Tense [will])

• After the tambourines dry, say/ask:

- "Decorate your tambourines with stickers and glitter." (Giving and Following Verbal Directives)
- "_____ is putting pretty stickers on his/her tambourine." (Present Tense Verbs)
- "Which stickers do you like?" (Questions [asking and/or responding])

• After the paint has dried on all of the tambourines, brush each one with a coat of Mod Podge. This will give them a glossy sheen and prevent the paint from staining hands and clothing. This can be done by the children or by the classroom adults while the children are at naptime or some other activity.

Post-Activity

• Once the tambourines have completely dried, use them to beat during singing time.

- "Who remembers how we made our tambourines?" (Questions [asking and/or responding]; Sequencing Skills; Vocabulary Review)
- "_____ glued the paper plates together." (Past Tense Verbs)
- "I drew pictures on my tambourine." (Past Tense Verbs)

Suggestion

Have a recording session during which the children sing some of their favorite songs while keeping the beat with their homemade tambourines.

CONCENTRATION

Figure 4.8. Concentration.

√	COMMUNICATION SKILL	√	COMMUNICATION SKILL
√	Auxiliary Verbs	√	Pragmatics
√	Cognitive Skills	√	Present Progressive Tense
√	Commentary, Questioning, Requesting	√	Present Tense Verbs
√	Concept Development		Requesting Assistance
√	Future Tense (will)	√	Questions (asking and/or responding)
√	Giving and Following Verbal Directives	√	Sequencing Skills
√	Modals	√	Vocabulary Development
	Negation	√	Vocabulary Review
	Past Tense Verbs		

Time Needed for Activity: Approximately 20 to 30 minutes
Difficulty Level: #2
Suggested Concepts and Vocabulary:

- words for numerals found in a deck of playing cards
- alphabet letters found in a deck of playing cards
- most
- least

Materials:

- one deck of playing cards with the joker(s) taken out

Procedure:

1. In an orderly manner, spread all of the cards out on a table across several rows.
2. Each player gets a chance to turn over two cards to see if they match.
3. If the two cards match, the player who turned them over gets to keep them and take another turn. As long as the player gets matching cards, he/she may continue going again.
4. If a player turns over two cards and they are not the same, the next player takes a turn.

Small Talk Suggestions:
Pre-Activity

- Take out the deck of cards.

  ◦ "I have a deck of cards." (Vocabulary Development)
  ◦ "Who can guess what we are going to do?" (Modals; Questions [asking and/ or responding])
  ◦ "Do you like to play cards?" (Auxiliary Verbs; Questions [asking and/or responding])
  ◦ "Let's play a game of Concentration! It's easy to play and lots of fun!" (Commentary, Questioning, Requesting)
  ◦ "Would you like to play Concentration with me?" (Modals; Questions [asking and/or responding])

During the Activity

- Explain to the children how to play Concentration as they watch you neatly place all of the cards on the table in rows/columns.

  ◦ "First, I place all of the cards on the table, face-down." (Sequencing Skills, Giving and Following Verbal Directives)
  ◦ "Second, I will pick two cards." (Sequencing Skills; Future Tense [will]; Giving and Following Verbal Directives)
  ◦ "Are these cards the same or different?" (Vocabulary Development; Questions [asking and/or responding]; Concept Development)
  ◦ "They are the same!" Or "They are different." (Concept Development; Vocabulary Development)
  ◦ "Who will go next?" (Sequencing Skills; Questions [asking and/or responding])
  ◦ "_____ is picking two cards." (Present Progressive Tense)
  ◦ "Do you like this game?" (Commentary, Questioning, Requesting; Questions [asking and/or responding])

- ○ "What cards did _____ choose?" (Concept Development; Questions [asking and/or responding])
- ○ "_____ likes this game." (Present Tense Verbs)

- When there are no cards left on the table, say/ask:

  - ○ "Let's count our cards to see who has the most!" (Cognitive Skills)
  - ○ "Who has the most cards?" "Who has the least?" (Vocabulary Development; Cognitive Skills; Questions [asking and/or responding])

Post-Activity

- Have the children teach another child how to play Concentration. Find a child from another class to be the student, or plan to have the children teach the game to a child who was absent on the day the class learned the game.

  - ○ "Let's tell _____ what we played today." (Pragmatics; Vocabulary Review)
  - ○ "Let's teach _____ how to play Concentration. What did we do first, then second, and what did we do after that?" (Sequencing Skills; Questions [asking and/or responding])

Suggestions

- Do some language modeling for the child. With each of your turns, exclaim "the same" if you get a match or "different" if the cards do not match. If the child has not yet internalized this basic concept, try saying "same" or "different" as the child, himself/herself, turns the cards over. Do not feel compelled to have the child repeat it until you feel that she/he is ready. You may find that after hearing you model just a few times, the child may begin using the correct words without much or any prompting from you.
- Use this card game for number and letter recognition. As each player takes a turn, he/she must say the card name then declare if they are the same or different.
- When all of the cards are gone from the table, help the child count all the winnings. The player with the most cards is the winner.
- Look for opportunities to vocally highlight specific vocabulary words throughout the activity, such as: playing cards, deck, deal, ace, king, queen, jack, heart, club, spade, diamond.

PENCIL HOLDER

Figure 4.9.   Pencil Holder.

√	COMMUNICATION SKILL	√	COMMUNICATION SKILL
√	Auxiliary Verbs	√	Pragmatics
√	Cognitive Skills	√	Present Progressive Tense
√	Commentary, Questioning, Requesting	√	Present Tense Verbs
√	Concept Development		Requesting Assistance
	Future Tense (will)	√	Questions (asking and/or responding)
√	Giving and Following Verbal Directives	√	Sequencing Skills
√	Modals	√	Vocabulary Development
	Negation	√	Vocabulary Review
√	Past Tense Verbs		

Time Needed for Activity: Approximately 30 to 45 minutes
Difficulty Level: #2
Suggested Concepts and Vocabulary:

- egg carton
- paint
- paintbrush
- paint pan

Materials:

- one cardboard egg carton
- tempura paints

- paintbrushes
- paint pans
- jars of clean water

Procedure:

1. With your child, select a paint color or a few different colors, and paint the egg carton.
2. Set the carton aside to dry completely.
3. Once the egg carton has dried, turn it over and poke small holes in each of the egg compartments for the child to store pens, pencils, thin felt-tipped markers, and scissors.

Small Talk Suggestions:
Pre-Activity

- Distribute the materials to each of the children.

  ○ "What did I bring in today?" (Vocabulary Development; Questions [asking and/or responding])
  ○ "Can you guess what we are doing today?" (Concept Development; Questions [asking and/or responding])

During the Activity

- Have a set of materials for the teacher. Instruct the children to follow the teacher's model.

  ○ "Do what I do." (Giving and Following Verbal Directives)
  ○ "_____ is punching the holes." (Present Progressive Tense)
  ○ "_____ enjoys painting." (Present Tense Verbs)
  ○ "Would you please pour some more paint, _____?" (Questions [asking and/or responding]; Commentary, Questioning, Requesting)
  ○ "_____ is decorating his/her pencil holder with stickers!" (Present Progressive Tense)
  ○ "_____ paints nicely." (Present Tense Verbs)
  ○ "What color(s) did you paint your pencil holder?" (Questions [asking and/or responding]; Concept Development; Cognitive Skills)
  ○ "Would you show me how to decorate my pencil holder, _____?" (Modals; Questions [asking and/or responding]; Commentary, Questioning, Requesting)

Post-Activity

- During the activity wrap-up or at Circle Time say/ask:
  - "Did you enjoy our activity today?" (Questions [asking and/or responding]; Commentary, Questioning, Requesting)
  - "What did we make?" (Questions [asking and/or responding]; Auxiliary Verbs; Vocabulary Review)
  - "_____ made a very pretty pencil holder." (Past Tense Verbs)
  - "What else can our pencil holders hold for us?" (Questions [asking and/or responding]; Modals; Vocabulary Development)
  - "Would you like to help someone else make a pencil holder?" (Questions [asking and/or responding])
  - "Tell _____ how to make a pencil holder." (Sequencing Skills; Pragmatics)

Suggestion

Some children in the class will likely be receiving services from the speech-language specialist. Establish a relationship with this professional for the benefit of the children. If symptoms of a language impairment present, it is imperative that the speech-language specialist be notified as soon as possible. Be prepared to report specific symptoms that have been observed in the classroom. This professional will know the appropriate assessments to perform and what therapeutic procedures should be put in place.

MAKE A CATERPILLAR

Figure 4.10.   Make a Caterpillar.

√	COMMUNICATION SKILL	√	COMMUNICATION SKILL
√	Auxiliary Verbs		Pragmatics
√	Cognitive Skills	√	Present Progressive Tense
	Commentary, Questioning, Requesting	√	Present Tense Verbs
√	Concept Development		Requesting Assistance
√	Future Tense (will)	√	Questions (asking and/or responding)
√	Giving and Following Verbal Directives		Sequencing Skills
√	Modals	√	Vocabulary Development
√	Negation	√	Vocabulary Review
√	Past Tense Verbs		

Time Needed for Activity: Approximately 1 hour
Difficulty Level: #2
Suggested Concepts and Vocabulary:

- caterpillar
- butterfly
- cocoon
- egg carton
- scissors
- cut
- paint

Materials:

- the bottom half of a cardboard egg carton for each participant
- tempura paints
- felt-tipped markers
- scissors
- stickers
- pipe cleaners

Procedure:

1. Cut the bottom portion of the egg carton in half, lengthwise.
2. Turn the egg compartment upside down, and let the child paint the outside any color or colors he/she chooses. Make colorful stickers available, too.
3. When the paint dries, help your child draw a face on one end of the egg carton.
4. Cut two 2-inch lengths of the pipe cleaner to fashion a pair of antennae for the new caterpillar.

Small Talk Suggestions:
Pre-Activity

- Consider starting this activity by reading *The Very Hungry Caterpillar* to the children, and have a completed egg carton caterpillar available to show.

  ○ "Look at what I made. What do you think this is?" (Questions [asking and/or responding]; Vocabulary Development)
  ○ "Do you want to make your own caterpillar?" (Questions [asking and/or responding]; Auxiliary Verbs)
  ○ "Would you like to make your own caterpillar?" (Questions [asking and/or responding]; Modals)
  ○ "Look at my caterpillar. What do you think you will need to make your caterpillar?" (Giving and Following Verbal Directives; Future Tense [will]; Questions [asking and/or responding]; Vocabulary Development)

- As the children list the supplies needed to make their caterpillars, ask a different child to retrieve each list item.

  ○ "_____, please get the _____." (Vocabulary Development; Giving and Following Verbal Directives)
  ○ "_____, please tell _____ what we need to make our caterpillars." (Vocabulary Development; Giving and Following Verbal Directives)

During the Activity

- The teacher should make another caterpillar along with the children in order to model the necessary steps in the process.
    - "I am cutting my egg carton in half." (Present Progressive Tense)
    - "I like how _____ cuts his/her egg carton in half." (Present Tense Verbs)
    - "What color will you paint your caterpillar?" (Questions [asking and/or responding]; Future Tense [will]; Concept Development)
    - "I will paint my caterpillar yellow." (Future Tense [will]; Concept Development)
    - "_____ is painting his/her caterpillar green." (Present Progressive Tense; Concept Development)
    - "_____ is drawing eyes on his/her caterpillar." (Present Progressive Tense; Vocabulary Development)
    - "How many eyes does a caterpillar have?" (Questions [asking and/or responding]; Concept Development)
    - "I am cutting two pieces of pipe cleaner to make the antennae." (Present Progressive Tense; Vocabulary Development)
    - "I like how _____ cuts the pipe cleaners." (Present Tense Verbs)

Post-Activity

- For Discussion/Circle Time:
    - "I painted my caterpillar yellow." (Past Tense Verbs; Vocabulary Review)
    - "I did not paint my caterpillar pink." (Negation; Vocabulary Review)
    - "What will the caterpillar make for its long sleep?" (Vocabulary Development; Vocabulary Review; Questions [asking and/or responding])
    - "What will a caterpillar turn into?" (Questions [asking and/or responding]; Future Tense [will]; Vocabulary Development; Vocabulary Review; Cognitive Skills)

Suggestions

- If a child is showing evidence of having problems comprehending verbal directives in the classroom, the teacher might try reducing her/his rate of speech. Some children require additional processing time as they listen to information pertaining to curriculum content. Understanding what they hear may require more time, but also these same children may need more processing time to generate a response to questions by the teacher.
- If a child in the class is having difficulty comprehending parts of the curriculum content, try working with the speech-language specialist to see if she/he might incorporate some of that content into therapy. The child will be receiving the needed speech-language therapy as well as getting extra help with what she/he may be struggling with in the classroom.

POP ART

Figure 4.11.   Pop Art.

√	COMMUNICATION SKILL	√	COMMUNICATION SKILL
√	Auxiliary Verbs		Pragmatics
√	Cognitive Skills	√	Present Progressive Tense
	Commentary, Questioning, Requesting	√	Present Tense Verbs
	Concept Development		Requesting Assistance
√	Future Tense (will)	√	Questions (asking and/or responding)
	Giving and Following Verbal Directives		Sequencing Skills
	Modals	√	Vocabulary Development
√	Negation	√	Vocabulary Review
√	Past Tense Verbs		

Time Needed for Activity: Approximately 30 to 40 minutes
Difficulty Level: #2
Suggested Concepts and Vocabulary:

- popcorn
- glue
- words for the various items drawn in outline for the children to fill in with popcorn

Materials:

- large bag of popcorn
- individual bowls for each activity participant

- rubber cement or Elmer's glue
- construction paper

Procedure:

1. For each child and adult participating in the activity, use a black felt-tip marker to draw the outline of an item that is familiar to the children, such as an animal, a flower, a letter of the alphabet or initial of the child's first name, a number (maybe the child's age), etc.
2. Give each participant a sheet of construction paper with a selected drawing on it.
3. Fill in each child's drawing with a sufficient amount of glue, smeared within the drawn outline.
4. Show the children how to take the pieces of popcorn and glue each bit to the area within the drawn outline.
5. Instruct the children to continue adding popcorn until their entire picture has been completely filled in.

Small Talk Suggestions:
Pre-Activity

- Show the children all of the materials for the activity.

  ○ "Who can guess what we will be doing with these things today?" (Questions [asking and/or responding]; Vocabulary Development)
  ○ "What will we do with these things?" (Future Tense [will])
  ○ "We are making art pictures with popcorn!" (Present Progressive Tense; Vocabulary Development)
  ○ "We will make popcorn art!" (Future Tense [will])

During the Activity

- Engage the children in the activity. Perform the steps of the activity, and talk about each step. Provide a narration.

  ○ "I am putting some glue all over the inside of my picture." (Present Progressive Tense)
  ○ "_____ is smearing the glue inside of his/her picture outline." (Present Progressive Tense)
  ○ "_____ smears the glue." (Present Tense Verbs)
  ○ "Wow! _____ is not smearing glue outside of the black line!" (Negation)
  ○ "Do you need more glue?" (Auxiliary Verbs)

- Wait for the children to complete the glue step, then let them see the teacher taking individual bits of popcorn from the bowl and placing it within the black picture outline.

  - "I am putting popcorn in my picture." (Present Progressive Tense)
  - "_____ drops the popcorn in the glue." (Present Tense Verbs)
  - "I think _____ is making a nice picture of a (item)." (Present Progressive Tense)

Post-Activity

- When the pictures are all filled in with popcorn, set them aside to dry as the children discuss the activity.

  - "What did we use to make our pictures?" (Vocabulary Review)
  - "What else can we do with popcorn?" (Questions [asking and/or responding]; Cognitive Skills)
  - "What else did we use for our popcorn art today?" (Vocabulary Review)
  - "I drew an outline of an object, and you filled it in with popcorn." (Past Tense Verbs)
  - "If we did not have any popcorn, what else could we have used instead of popcorn?" (Cognitive Skills; Questions [asking and/or responding])

Suggestion

Instead of purchasing a bag of ready-made popcorn for this activity, try obtaining a container of popcorn kernels, and make the popcorn either in the school kitchen or, where permissible, in a classroom microwave. Get the children to guess how many minutes it will take for the first popcorn kernel to POP!

CHALLENGING ACTIVITIES

These activities (Difficulty Level #3) may require more than usual hand-over-hand assistance with children who possess little experience handling arts and crafts and/or cooking and eating utensils.

INDOOR PLANTER

Figure 5.1A.   Indoor Planter A.

Figure 5.1B.   Indoor Planter B.

Figure 5.1C.   Indoor Planter C.

√	COMMUNICATION SKILL	√	COMMUNICATION SKILL
√	Auxiliary Verbs		Pragmatics
√	Cognitive Skills	√	Present Progressive Tense
√	Commentary, Questioning, Requesting		Present Tense Verbs
√	Concept Development	√	Requesting Assistance
√	Future Tense (will)	√	Questions (asking and/or responding)
√	Giving and Following Verbal Directives		Sequencing Skills
√	Modals	√	Vocabulary Development
	Negation	√	Vocabulary Review
	Past Tense Verbs		

Time Needed for Activity: Approximately 45 minutes
Difficulty Level: #3
Suggested Concepts and Vocabulary:

- planter box
- dirt/soil
- root
- jar
- seed
- paper
- moisten

Materials:

- one empty baby food jar or any other type of small jar for each child
- potting soil to fill the jars almost to the top
- a 2-inch square piece of paper (a light-colored piece of construction paper, such as yellow or pink)
- any kind of large seed (perhaps a string bean seed)

Procedure:

1. Moisten the paper.
2. Place the seed against the side of the jar, and hold it in place with the moist paper.
3. Fill the jar with the potting soil, and be certain that you pack enough soil to keep the paper and seed in place against the side of the jar.
4. Lightly moisten the soil.
5. Over the next few days, watch the seed grow with your child. Point out to your child how the root starts to grow downward as the plant stem begins to climb upward and out of the jar.

Small Talk Suggestions:
Pre-Activity

- Show the children a finished model of an indoor planter wherein a plant has already started to grow.

  - "Boys and girls, what do you think we are going to do today?" (Questions [asking and/or responding]; Cognitive Skills)
  - Look at my planter, and tell me what you think we need for our activity." (Vocabulary Development)

- "What kind of food will grow from a string been seed?" (Questions [asking and/or responding]; Cognitive Skills)
- "Is a string bean a fruit or a vegetable?" (Questions [asking and/or responding]; Concept Development; Cognitive Skills)
- "What color will our string bean be?" (Questions [asking and/or responding]; Concept Development)
- "What other food is green?" (Concept Development; Cognitive Skills)
- "Who likes to eat string beans at home?" (Questions [asking and/or responding])
- "Do you like vegetables?" (Auxiliary Verbs)

- As the teacher names the items needed for the activity, the children must look around for the items, and bring them to the table.

  - "Now, we need jars for everyone (the bag of soil, small pieces of paper, etc.)" (Vocabulary Development; Giving and Following Verbal Directives)

During the Activity

- Make the children active participants in the activity process.

  - "Can you help me give out the jars for everyone?" (Modals; Requesting Assistance)
  - "_____ can count how many seeds we will need." (Concept Development; Future Tense [will]; Modals)
  - "Moisten your string bean seed in some water." (Giving and Following Verbal Directives)
  - "Help me pour some soil in the jars." (Giving and Following Verbal Directives)
  - "Who is pouring soil?" (Questions [asking and/or responding]; Present Progressive Tense)
  - "Let's put our string bean plants on the windowsill." (Giving and Following Verbal Directives)
  - "Why should we put our plants on the windowsill? What do our string bean plants need?" (Questions [asking and/or responding]; Cognitive Skills)

Post-Activity

- Stimulate a discussion about the indoor planter.

  - "What did you like most about making our indoor planter?" (Questions [asking and/or responding]; Commentary, Questioning, Requesting; Vocabulary Development; Vocabulary Review)
  - "Who did not like making the planter? Tell me why." (Questions [asking and/or responding]; Commentary, Questioning, Requesting; Vocabulary Development; Vocabulary Review)

- ○ "What other plants grow from seeds?" (Questions [asking and/or responding]; Cognitive Skills; Vocabulary Development; Vocabulary Review)
- ○ "What flowers grow from seeds?" (Questions [asking and/or responding]; Cognitive Skills; Vocabulary Development; Vocabulary Review)
- ○ "When we make another planter, should we plant another vegetable?" (Questions [asking and/or responding]; Modals; Vocabulary Development; Vocabulary Review)
- ○ "Should we plant a flower seed one day?" (Questions [asking and/or responding]; Modals; Vocabulary Development; Vocabulary Review)
- ○ "What will we need when we plant another seed?" (Questions [asking and/or responding]; Future Tense [will]; Vocabulary Review)
- ○ "What will happen if we forget to water our seeds?" (Questions [asking and/or responding]; Cognitive Skills; Vocabulary Development; Vocabulary Review)

Suggestions

- As the plant develops, alert the children to the root that starts growing from the seed. Show the children how the root grows downward toward the soil while the stem starts its journey upward. Every now and then, view the bottom of the jar to see how the root system develops.
- Perform the same activity with different types of seeds, such as flower seeds and other vegetable seeds.

MAKE A DRUM

Figure 5.2.   Make a Drum.

√	COMMUNICATION SKILL	√	COMMUNICATION SKILL
√	Auxiliary Verbs		Pragmatics
	Cognitive Skills	√	Present Progressive Tense
√	Commentary, Questioning, Requesting	√	Present Tense Verbs
	Concept Development		Requesting Assistance
√	Future Tense (will)	√	Questions (asking and/or responding)
√	Giving and Following Verbal Directives	√	Sequencing Skills
√	Modals	√	Vocabulary Development
√	Negation	√	Vocabulary Review
√	Past Tense Verbs		

Time Needed for Activity: Approximately 1 hour
Difficulty Level: #3
Suggested Concepts and Vocabulary:

- box
- rubber band
- drumsticks
- paint
- balloon

Materials:

- empty Quaker Oats or hominy grits boxes for each child (the type made from paper) or an empty coffee can for each participant
- construction paper
- rubber bands (2 per child)
- pencils for drumsticks (2 per child)
- tempera paints or colorful stickers or glitter and glue for drum decorations
- 2 balloons for each participant

Procedure:

1. Throw away the container's lid.
2. Cut out the entire bottom of the container. Use a can opener if using coffee cans.
3. Cut construction paper to the length of the container, then wrap it around the Quaker Oats box or coffee can and secure it with tape.
4. Decorate the construction paper with stickers, paints, glitter, or whatever the children select. Alternatively, it might be a good idea to have the children decorate one side of a sheet of construction paper that has been precut to the size of a container. The decorated paper can, then, be wrapped around the container and securely taped in place.
5. Use scissors to cut off about a half inch of the balloon at the stem.
6. Stretch a balloon over each end of the box. Adults may need to perform this step for the children.
7. Secure the balloons with a rubber band on each end of the box. You can use tape over the rubber bands to make them more secure.
8. Now, the drum is completed. Use the eraser end of two pencils as drumsticks. For safety, pencils that have not yet been sharpened are highly recommended.

Small Talk Suggestions:
Pre-Activity

- Set the materials out on a table for all the children to view.
  - "Guess what we are making today." (Commentary, Questioning, Requesting)
  - "Who likes the sound of drums?" (Questions [asking and/or responding]; Present Tense Verbs)
  - "Tell me what you see on the table." (Vocabulary Development)

During the Activity

- Engage the children in the activity.
  - "Ask _____ for a container (two balloons, two rubber bands, stickers, etc.)." (Giving and Following Verbal Directives)
  - "_____ likes interesting stickers." (Present Tense Verbs; Commentary, Questioning, Requesting)
  - "Do you like drums?" (Questions [asking and/or responding]; Auxiliary Verbs)
  - "Can you play drums?" (Questions [asking and/or responding]; Modals)
  - "_____ is stretching the balloon over his/her container." (Present Progressive Tense)
  - "Will we beat our drums when we sing songs?" (Questions [asking and/or responding]; Future Tense [will])

- Once the drums have been completed, say/ask:
  - "What songs should we sing while we beat our drums?" (Future Tense [will]; Modals)
  - "Do you like to play the drums?" (Questions [asking and/or responding]; Auxiliary Verbs)
  - "_____ is singing and drumming!" (Present Progressive Tense)

Post-Activity

- Wrap up the activity with a discussion about the drums.
  - "So, what did we do today?" (Questions [asking and/or responding]; Past Tense Verbs)
  - "Did we beat the drums?" (Questions [asking and/or responding]; Auxiliary Verbs)
  - "Oh, _____ did not like making a drum today. Why?" (Questions [asking and/or responding]; Negation; Commentary, Questioning, Requesting)
  - "Let's tell Ms./Mr. _____ how we made our drums." (Sequencing Skills; Vocabulary Review)

Suggestion

Have a recording session during which the children sing some of their favorite songs while keeping the beat with their homemade drums.

GO FISH

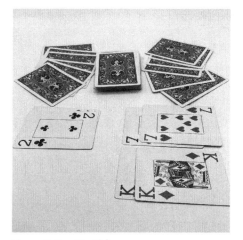

Figure 5.3.   Go Fish.

√	COMMUNICATION SKILL	√	COMMUNICATION SKILL
√	Auxiliary Verbs		Pragmatics
	Cognitive Skills	√	Present Progressive Tense
√	Commentary, Questioning, Requesting		Present Tense Verbs
√	Concept Development		Requesting Assistance
	Future Tense (will)	√	Questions (asking and/or responding)
	Giving and Following Verbal Directives	√	Sequencing Skills
√	Modals		Vocabulary Development
√	Negation		Vocabulary Review
	Past Tense Verbs		

Time Needed for Activity: Approximately 15 to 20 minutes
Difficulty Level: #3
Suggested Concepts and Vocabulary:

- words for numerals found in a deck of playing cards
- alphabet letters found in a deck of playing cards

Materials:

- one deck of playing cards, preferably with large numbers and letters

Object of the Game:

The object of Go Fish is to be the player who has the most pairs after all the cards have been paired.

Procedure:

1. Remove the joker card(s), and shuffle the entire remaining deck.
2. Deal six cards to each player, and place the remaining cards face-down between the players.
3. To start the game, each player must look over all his/her cards in search of pairs, such as two queens, two nines, two aces, etc. If a pair is found, the player takes it out of his/her hand and places it on the table in front of him/her, face-up. If another pair is found, the player must place it on the table next to the previous pair. Players should keep looking until all pairs are found and placed on the table.
4. Any unpaired cards that remain in a player's hand need to get a match. When it is a player's turn, she/he should look at his/her cards to find a card that needs a match, such as a ten. The player must pick a different player and ask, "Do you have a ten? If the player who was asked has a ten, he/she must give it to the player who asked for it. The player who did the asking takes the ten and pairs it on the table with the ten that he/she already had. That player then gets to go again, picking a player and trying to make another match. If the player being asked does not have the requested card, then that player must say, "No, go fish." The player whose turn it is then picks a card from the deck that is face-down in the middle of the table. If she/he gets a match, then that pair is put down on the table, and the player goes again. If a match is not made, the new card drawn is placed in with the other cards in the player's hand, and the next player goes.
5. If only two people are playing, the game is over after one player runs out of cards. If three to five people are playing, the game is over after all pairs have been matched. All players then count how many pairs they have. The player with the most pairs is the winner.

Small Talk Suggestions:
Pre-Activity

- Show the card deck to the children.
  - "Can you guess what we are going to play?" (Questions [asking and/or responding]; Modals)
  - "Each person gets six cards. Let's count together." (Concept Development)

During the Activity

- As the card game progresses, use appropriate opportunities to comment and question. For example:

  ○ Child: Do you have a six?

  Teacher: _____ is asking for the number six. (Auxiliary Verbs; Present Progressive Tense)

  OR

  Teacher: No, I don't have a six. Go fish. (Negation)

  OR

  Teacher: _____ and _____ are playing Go Fish! (Present Progressive Tense)

Post-Activity

- Discuss the activity immediately following the card game.

  ○ "Did you enjoy playing Go Fish?" (Auxiliary Verbs; Commentary, Questioning, Requesting)
  ○ "What other card game do you play?" (Commentary, Questioning, Requesting)
  ○ "Let's teach Ms./Mr. _____ how to play Go Fish!" (Sequencing Skills)

Suggestions

- If the child is unable to identify cards in his hand when asked for a specific card, try holding up the card you are requesting as you ask for it, using its label. For example, if you wish to request a king, hold up the king as you ask, "Do you have a king?" Do this throughout play. Eventually the child will associate the card with the number or name.
- If you are teaching question forms, use this card game while vocally highlighting the question pattern, "Do you have a _____?"
- Go Fish, as well as other card and board games, can be useful in teaching conversational turn-taking. In order for the child to fully participate in the game, he/she must wait for his/her turn, not only for when to pick a card but also for when to utter the phrases required in this game.
- When playing with more than two people, it might be a good idea to have the children start their turns with the player to the left of the dealer. This can be a good way to develop left-right discrimination.
- If you are working on the development of specific speech-sound production, review this card game before engaging the child in it to see if any of the sounds

that need development in the child's speech are used in this game. If so, when it is your turn to use a phrase containing that sound, vocally highlight the word with that sound as a way of modeling articulation for the child. As the game progresses, he/she will undoubtedly have ample opportunity to practice this sound within the process of playing the card game.

- Look for opportunities to vocally highlight specific vocabulary words throughout the activity, such as: playing cards, deck, deal, ace, king, queen, jack, heart, club, spade, diamond.

SPONGE PAINTINGS

Figure 5.4.   Sponge Painting.

√	COMMUNICATION SKILL	√	COMMUNICATION SKILL
	Auxiliary Verbs		Pragmatics
√	Cognitive Skills	√	Present Progressive Tense
√	Commentary, Questioning, Requesting		Present Tense Verbs
√	Concept Development	√	Requesting Assistance
√	Future Tense (will)	√	Questions (asking and/or responding)
√	Giving and Following Verbal Directives		Sequencing Skills
√	Modals	√	Vocabulary Development
√	Negation	√	Vocabulary Review
√	Past Tense Verbs		

Time Needed for Activity: Approximately 30 to 45 minutes
Difficulty Level: #3
Suggested Concepts and Vocabulary:

- sponge
- decoration

Materials:

- an assortment of tempura paint colors
- a dry sponge cut into approximately 1-inch squares (one for each paint color)
- construction paper
- small paint dishes for each paint color

Procedure:

1. Pour a different color paint into each of the paint dishes.
2. Help your child to lightly dip a sponge into the paint.
3. Make a variety of designs on the construction paper by lightly touching/tapping the sponge to the paper.

Note: Avoid drenching the sponge with paint. The drier and stiffer the sponge, the more distinct the design.

Small Talk Suggestions:
Pre-Activity

- Show the children examples of sponge paintings that the teachers have completed.

  ○ "How do you think I made these pictures?" (Questions [asking and/or responding]; Cognitive Skills; Commentary, Questioning, Requesting; Vocabulary Development)
  ○ "I did not use a paintbrush brush." (Negation; Vocabulary Development)
  ○ "I didn't use my fingers like in finger-painting." (Negation)
  ○ "I used sponges!" (Past Tense Verbs)
  ○ "What do you use sponges for around the house and in school?" (Questions [asking and/or responding]; Cognitive Skills)
  ○ "I will cut up some sponges for us to make our sponge pictures!" (Future Tense [will])
  ○ "Who will get the construction paper for us?" (Questions [asking and/or responding]; Future Tense [will])
  ○ "Who will get the paints for us?" (Questions [asking and/or responding]; Future Tense [will])
  ○ "_____, please get the paint dishes for us." (Requesting Assistance)

During the Activity

- As the children follow the teacher's example, say/ask:

  ○ "Watch me carefully use a sponge to gently dip into a color. What color am I using?" (Concept Development; Giving and Following Verbal Directives)
  ○ "I am carefully touching my paper with the colored sponge to make decorations all over my paper." (Present Progressive Tense)
  ○ "_____ is decorating his/her paper." (Present Progressive Tense)
  ○ "What color is _____ using?" (Questions [asking and/or responding]; Present Progressive Tense)
  ○ "Maybe _____ will choose a different color next." (Future Tense [will])

Post-Activity

- As the dried sponge paintings are being hung up for display, ask:

  ○ "What did we do with paint and sponges?" (Questions [asking and/or responding]; Vocabulary Review)
  ○ "Would you like to do this again one day?" (Questions [asking and/or responding]; Modals)
  ○ "What else can we use to create pictures with our paint?" (Questions [asking and/or responding]; Vocabulary Review)

Suggestion

Be as observant as possible regarding the child's interest in the conversation. If the child is giving inappropriate responses during a conversation, is staring into space, or the adult must frequently repeat the question or comment, it might be better to politely end the conversation and try again some other time. The child's behavior may not be indicative of a language problem. It may possible that the child is bored, hungry, or not interested in the topic.

CORNCOB PAINTINGS

Figure 5.5.   Corn Cob Picture.

√	COMMUNICATION SKILL	√	COMMUNICATION SKILL
√	Auxiliary Verbs		Pragmatics
√	Cognitive Skills		Present Progressive Tense
√	Commentary, Questioning, Requesting		Present Tense Verbs
	Concept Development		Requesting Assistance
√	Future Tense (will)	√	Questions (asking and/or responding)
√	Giving and Following Verbal Directives	√	Sequencing Skills
√	Modals	√	Vocabulary Development
√	Negation	√	Vocabulary Review
√	Past Tense Verbs		

Time Needed for Activity: Approximately 30 to 45 minutes
Difficulty Level: #3
Suggested Concepts and Vocabulary:

- corn
- corncob

Materials:

- tempera paints
- an aluminum pie tin for each color to be used
- dried corncob (without the kernels and about 2 to 3 inches in length)
- a large sheet of construction paper

Procedure:

1. Pour a small amount of paint into each of the pie tins.
2. Lightly tap a corncob in the paint.
3. Gently roll or press the corncob on the sheet of paper to make a design.
4. Do the same for any other color that the child desires.

Small Talk Suggestions:
Pre-Activity

- Make several corncob paintings with a variety of colors on construction paper, then display them prominently within the children's view.

  - "Oh, these are my corncob paintings." (Commentary, Questioning, Requesting; Vocabulary Development)
  - "I did not use a paintbrush to make them." (Negation)
  - "What do you think I used to make my corncob paintings?" (Questions [asking and/or responding]; Cognitive Skills)
  - "Would you like to make a corncob painting?" (Questions [asking and/or responding]; Modals)
  - "Tell me what you think we will need for our corncob paintings." (Cognitive Skills; Future Tense [will])

During the Activity

- Put one child in charge of the supplies, and direct the children to address that child for the art supplies.

  - "Politely ask _____ for the paints (and other materials)." (Giving and Following Verbal Directives)

- One by one, permit the children to direct the activity.

  - "Okay, _____, tell me what to do next." (Sequencing Skills; Vocabulary Development; Giving and Following Verbal Directives)

Post-Activity

- During Discussion/Circle Time:

  - "All of you painted beautiful corncob pictures!" (Past Tense Verbs)
  - "How did you make such nice paintings?" (Questions [asking and/or responding]; Vocabulary Review)

○ "Do you want to do this again one day?" (Questions [asking and/or responding]; Auxiliary Verbs)

Suggestion

Talk with the children about other uses for corn, such as using corn kernels for making popcorn or for food to feed farm animals, and using cornmeal to make corn bread or corn muffins.

STRING PICTURE

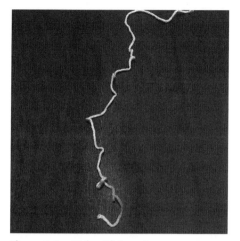

Figure 5.6.   String Picture A.

Figure 5.7.   String Picture B.

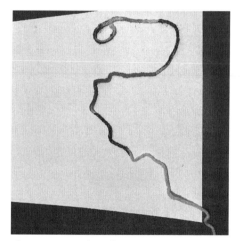

Figure 5.8.   String Picture C.

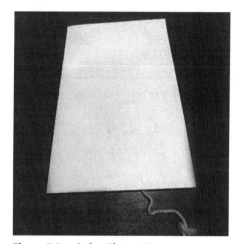

Figure 5.9.   String Picture D.

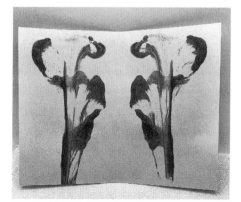

Figure 5.10.   String Picture E.

√	COMMUNICATION SKILL	√	COMMUNICATION SKILL
	Auxiliary Verbs	√	Pragmatics
	Cognitive Skills	√	Present Progressive Tense
	Commentary, Questioning, Requesting	√	Present Tense Verbs
	Concept Development		Requesting Assistance
	Future Tense (will)	√	Questions (asking and/or responding)
√	Giving and Following Verbal Directives	√	Sequencing Skills
√	Modals	√	Vocabulary Development
	Negation	√	Vocabulary Review
√	Past Tense Verbs		

Time Needed for Activity: Approximately 30 to 45 minutes
Difficulty Level: #3
Suggested Concepts and Vocabulary:

- string, yarn
- scissors
- cut

Materials:

- ball of yarn (String can be used, but yarn is preferable as it soaks up more paint than string.)
- tempera paints
- paintbrushes
- white construction paper
- scissors

Procedure:

1. Give each participant a sheet of white construction paper.
2. Fold the paper in half, then place it aside.
3. Cut about an arm's length (the child's arm as a measure) of yarn for each participant. See figure 5.6.
4. Spread some newspaper on the table, and instruct each participant to place her/his length of yarn on the newspaper.
5. Using the paintbrushes, paint each inch of the yarn with a different color, but leave about a half inch at the end unpainted. See figure 5.7.
6. On one side of the folded white construction paper, place the painted yarn in any desired configuration, but be mindful to let the unpainted portion of yarn hang off the paper. See figure 5.8.

7. Fold the paper over the side with the painted yarn, and press the weight of a hand or book evenly over the folded paper. See figure 5.9.
8. Grab the unpainted piece of yarn, and slowly pull it free from the folded paper.
9. Discard the used yarn.
10. Open the white construction paper, and admire the beautiful work of art!!! See figure 5.10.
11. Let it dry, then display.

Small Talk Suggestions:
Pre-Activity

- Show each of the activity supplies to the children.
  - "Who can tell me what this is?" (Questions [asking and/or responding])
  - "What is this, _____?" (Questions [asking and/or responding]; Vocabulary Development)
  - "Can you guess what we will make with these things?" (Questions [asking and/or responding]; Modals)
  - "What is made from yarn?" (Questions [asking and/or responding]; Vocabulary Development)

During the Activity

- Model the activity actions for the children.
  - "_____ is cutting some yarn." (Present Progressive Tense)
  - "_____ cuts a long piece of yarn." (Present Tense Verbs)
  - "Be careful with your scissors." (Giving and Following Verbal Directives)
  - "Who wants the paint now?" (Questions [asking and/or responding]; Present Tense Verbs)
  - "_____ is painting the yarn with pretty colors." (Present Progressive Tense)
  - "What will you do with the paints?" (Questions [asking and/or responding])
  - "Can you cut some more yarn for me, please?" (Questions [asking and/or responding]; Modals)

Post-Activity

- Talk about the activity as the teacher puts the yarn pictures on the display wall.
  - "What did we do today?" (Questions [asking and/or responding]; Vocabulary Review)
  - "What did we do first?" (Questions [asking and/or responding]; Sequencing Skills)

- ○ "What did we do last?" (Questions [asking and/or responding]; Sequencing Skills)
- ○ "_____ pulled the yarn through the folded paper." (Questions [asking and/or responding]; Past Tense Verbs)
- ○ "_____ painted her/his yarn different colors." (Past Tense Verbs)
- ○ "_____ painted her/his yarn with only three colors." (Past Tense Verbs)
- ○ "Let's tell _____ what we did today." (Pragmatics; Sequencing Skills)

Suggestion

Sponsor an art workshop for the children to conduct for another class. Let the children who are familiar with string art teach the workshop participants the procedure for creating pictures with string or yarn, paint, and construction paper.

VASE

Figure 5.11.   Vase.

√	COMMUNICATION SKILL	√	COMMUNICATION SKILL
	Auxiliary Verbs	√	Pragmatics
√	Cognitive Skills	√	Present Progressive Tense
√	Commentary, Questioning, Requesting	√	Present Tense Verbs
√	Concept Development		Requesting Assistance
√	Future Tense (will)	√	Questions (asking and/or responding)
√	Giving and Following Verbal Directives	√	Sequencing Skills
√	Modals	√	Vocabulary Development
	Negation	√	Vocabulary Review
√	Past Tense Verbs		

Time Needed for Activity: Approximately 1 hour
Difficulty Level: #3
Suggested Concepts and Vocabulary:

- masking tape
- bottle
- shoe polish
- rub
- rag

Materials:

- A 20-fluid ounce soda bottle for each child (clean and dry, inside and out)
- rolls of masking tape for each child (or a roll for every pair of children to share)

- brown shoe polish
- cloth rags
- a shoe polish applicator
- appropriately sized nitrile gloves for each participant (Latex gloves are not recommended, as some children may be allergic to them.)
- long-stemmed flowers (real or artificial)

Procedure:

1. Tear off a piece of masking tape, and stick it to the bottle. Pieces can be about one square inch. Some pieces can be larger or smaller. Edges can be a variety of smooth and jagged.
2. Cover the entire outside of the bottle with the pieces of masking tape.
3. Use the shoe polish applicator to lightly dab the brown shoe polish, then rub some onto the bottle for each participant. Smear the brown shoe polish all over the bottle. A tiny amount should be just enough to color the bottle.
4. Use a clean rag to rub the brown shoe polish into the masking tape. A second clean rag will be needed to eliminate shoe polish residue from the bottle.
5. Continue rubbing the shoe polish until there is no residue on the masking tape, and the bottle can be handled without brown shoe polish marring hands and clothing. It is advisable that an adult complete the rubbing even after the child claims to be finished.
6. Place a long-stemmed flower in the bottle!

Small Talk Suggestions:
Pre-Activity

- Place a completed vase in a prominent location that will most likely be visible to the children. Put attractive, colorful flowers (real or artificial) in the vase to increase the interest of the children. Wait for the children to ask and/or comment about the new display. (Commentary, Questioning, Requesting)

  ○ "What are the flowers in?" (Questions [asking and/or responding]; Concept Development; Vocabulary Development)
  ○ "What will we need to make the flower vase?" (Questions [asking and/or responding]; Vocabulary Development)

- Instruct the children to ask a designated child to get the needed materials for the activity.

  ○ "Ask _____ to get the bottles/masking tape/brown shoe polish/rags/newspaper." (Questions [asking and/or responding]; Vocabulary Development)
  ○ "What should we put on the table to keep it clean?" (Questions [asking and/or responding]; Modals)

During the Activity

- Make a flower vase along with the children, but be certain to remain a step ahead of them in order to model the steps for the children.

    ○ "What do you think we will do with the masking tape?" (Questions [asking and/or responding]; Cognitive Skills)
    ○ "_____ is tearing off a piece of tape." (Present Progressive Tense)
    ○ "_____ tears off some tape." (Present Tense Verbs)
    ○ "What will you do with the masking tape?" (Questions [asking and/or responding]; Future Tense [will])
    ○ "We are sticking the tape to the bottle." (Present Progressive Tense)
    ○ "Put the tape on the bottle." (Giving and Following Verbal Directives)
    ○ "_____ is covering the bottle with masking tape." (Present Progressive Tense)
    ○ "Stick the tape to the top of the bottle and the bottom of the bottle." (Giving and Following Verbal Directives)

- Applying the brown shoe polish may require some hand-over-hand assistance for the children. Some, however, may have adequate fine motor control to complete this step of the activity.

    ○ "_____ is smearing a little bit of brown shoe polish on the bottle." (Present Progressive Tense)
    ○ "First, smear some brown shoe polish on each side of the bottle and on the bottom." (Sequencing Skills; Concept Development; Giving and Following Verbal Directives)
    ○ "_____ is using a clean rag to rub the polish into the tape on the bottle." (Present Progressive Tense; Concept Development)
    ○ "Use the rag to rub the polish all over the bottle." (Giving and Following Verbal Directives; Concept Development)
    ○ "Next, use another clean rag to rub off the extra polish." (Sequencing Skills; Concept Development)

- As the children finish rubbing off the excess shoe polish, be certain to move among the children with a clean rag to do some extra rubbing. The flower vase is complete when the vase has an aged look without brown polish rubbing off on one's hands.

    ○ "Are you finished?" (Questions [asking and/or responding]; Past Tense Verbs)
    ○ "What will we put in our flower vases?" (Questions [asking and/or responding]; Concept Development; Cognitive Skills; Vocabulary Review)
    ○ "_____ is placing a flower in his/her flower vase." (Present Progressive Tense)

Post-Activity

- Discussion/Circle Time:
    - "What did we make today?" (Questions [asking and/or responding]; Vocabulary Review)
    - "We made flower vases." (Commentary, Questioning, Requesting)
    - "What did we put in the vases?" (Questions [asking and/or responding]; Vocabulary Review)
    - "How did we make our flower vases?" (Questions [asking and/or responding]; Sequencing Skills; Vocabulary Review)
    - "What did we do first?" (Questions [asking and/or responding]; Sequencing Skills)
    - "What did we do next and after that?" (Questions [asking and/or responding]; Sequencing Skills)
    - "What did we do last?" (Questions [asking and/or responding]; Sequencing Skills)
    - "Let's tell _____ about our flower vases." (Pragmatics)

Suggestion

When a child is experiencing strong emotions about something that has happened in her/his life, it is a good idea for the teacher to reflect the child's feeling as best as possible. This might be a good time to show empathy with the child by providing her/him with the words that match the emotions at the time. For example, if the child has had a serious argument with another child, it might be apropos to say something like, "I bet you are very upset with Susie." Rephrasing/Restating what the angry child says is a good way to teach the child the appropriate words to express powerful feelings in a given situation.

HOPSCOTCH

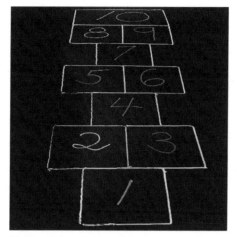

Figure 5.12.   Hopscotch.

√	COMMUNICATION SKILL	√	COMMUNICATION SKILL
	Auxiliary Verbs		Pragmatics
√	Cognitive Skills	√	Present Progressive Tense
	Commentary, Questioning, Requesting	√	Present Tense Verbs
√	Concept Development		Requesting Assistance
	Future Tense (will)	√	Questions (asking and/or responding)
√	Giving and Following Verbal Directives	√	Sequencing Skills
√	Modals		Vocabulary Development
	Negation		Vocabulary Review
√	Past Tense Verbs		

Time Needed for Activity: Approximately 30 to 45 minutes
Difficulty Level: #3
Suggested Concepts and Vocabulary:

- beanbag
- toss
- words for numerals associated with hopscotch game

Materials:

- a stick of chalk (any color)
- a small beanbag or small pebble/rock or a soda bottle cap (the marker or shooter)
- clear pavement (school yard)

Procedure:

1. Using the chalk, make a "gameboard" to look like the one pictured in figure 5.12.
2. The first child stands before square #1.
3. She/He must toss the marker into square #1. It has to land in the square without touching the lines or bouncing out of the box. It must land directly within the box, not on a line.
4. The child must hop through the course of squares, skipping over the first square where the marker rests. The single squares must be hopped on with only one foot. The side-by-side squares must be straddled, with one foot in the left square and the other foot in the right square.
5. After the child hops into the "rest" square, he/she can turn around and hop back to the starting point. When the child hops to the square where the marker rests, he/she has to carefully balance on one foot, pick up the marker, then hop all the way back to square #1. If the child hops the game course successfully both ways, he/she gets to toss the marker into the next square (square #2) and then follow the same procedure as with square #1.
6. If the child steps on the line, misses the correct square or steps into a square with both feet, or loses balance, his/her turn ends, and the next child goes.
7. Players begin their turn where they left off.
8. The hopscotch winner is the first child who completes the game course for each of the numbered squares.

Small Talk Suggestions:
Pre-Activity

- Gather the children together on the school's playground and show them the hopscotch playing course, or draw the hopscotch course as the children look on. Tell them the name of the game, and explain how the game is played.

  - "Who wants to play hopscotch?" (Questions [asking and/or responding]; Present Tense Verbs)
  - "Let's count the numbers together." (Cognitive Skills; Giving and Following Verbal Directives)
  - "How many hopscotch boxes do you see?" (Concept Development; Questions [asking and/or responding])
  - "Who will go first (second, third, last)?" (Concept Development; Questions [asking and/or responding])
  - "Can you hop?" (Modals; Questions [asking and/or responding])
  - "How are hopping and jumping the same?" (Cognitive Skills; Question [asking and/or responding])

- ○ "How are hopping and jumping different?" (Cognitive Skills; Question [asking and/or responding])

During the Activity

- The teacher should start the game in order to model the activity.
  - ○ "I am tossing the beanbag." (Present Progressive Tense)
  - ○ "What number did the beanbag land on?" (Questions [asking and/or responding]; Cognitive Skills; Concept Development)
  - ○ "Would you like to go next?" (Questions [asking and/or responding]; Modals; Sequencing Skills)
  - ○ "_____ is hopping." (Present Progressive Tense)

Post-Activity

- Once the game is over, talk about the activity. It might be a good idea to have the brief discussion within sight of the hopscotch course or with a picture available if the children must go indoors.
  - ○ "What was the name of the game we played?" (Questions [asking and/or responding]; Past Tense Verbs)
  - ○ "Should we play this game again one day?" (Questions [asking and/or responding]; Modals)
  - ○ "Could we play hopscotch without a beanbag?" (Questions [asking and/or responding]; Modals)

Suggestion

Be on the lookout for nonverbal communications cues from a child. Try to be aware of how a child is really feeling by being constantly aware of the child's vocal tone when speaking, posture, facial expression, energy level or lack of it, and her/his behavioral changes, if any. If the teacher detects that the child is having a bad day or something else may be interfering with the child's happiness and ability to learn, it may be a good idea to set aside a quiet place to speak with the child, and encourage her/him to talk about her/his feelings. The teacher could also use this time to do some restating and rephrasing as the child speaks. In this way, the teacher will demonstrate concern for the child and get information from the child to solve a possibly serious problem.

LETTER TO TEACHERS

Dear Teacher,

Thank you so much for your hard work and dedication to the education of our young learners. When people speak of "first responders," I often include teachers, who are at the forefront of preparing our kiddos for exciting futures. Also, thank you for using *Small Talk: Activities for Language Development in Preschool Learners*. It is hoped that the activities will be fun and engaging from start to finish. In fact, I would be delighted to see how the activities worked out for your class. If you would like, please send a photograph of some of the completed projects to taylorspeechandlanguage@gmail.com. Thank you!

Sincerely,
Reid Taylor

BIBLIOGRAPHY

American Speech-Language-Hearing Association. "Preschool Language Disorders." Accessed February 8, 2021, https://www.asha.org/public/speech/disorders/preschool-language-dis orders/#signs.

Centers for Disease Control and Prevention. "CDC's Developmental Milestones." June 10, 2020, https://www.cdc.gov/ncbddd/actearly/milestones/index.html.

ABOUT THE AUTHOR

Charles Reid Taylor is associate professor in the Special Education Department at New Jersey City University (NJCU). In addition to teaching at the university level, he provides diagnostic and therapeutic services as a speech-language pathologist in private practice. Prior to teaching undergraduate and graduate courses at NJCU, Dr. Taylor worked as a speech-language specialist at the A. Harry Moore Laboratory School, a department of NJCU devoted to the education of children presenting with physical and developmental disabilities.